Also by Jenny La Sala

My Family Compass

Comes A Soldier's Whisper

Vietnam and Beyond, Veteran Reflections

When Daddy Comes Home

NEVER FORGOTTEN

THE VIETNAM VETERAN FIFTY YEARS LATER

Jenny La Sala

Order this book online at www.trafford.com
or email orders@trafford.com

Most Trafford titles are also available at major online book retailers.

Print information available on the last page.

ISBN: 978-1-4907-6642-3 (sc)
ISBN: 978-1-4907-6641-6 (hc)
ISBN: 978-1-4907-6650-8 (e)

Library of Congress Control Number: 2015917635

Trafford rev. 02/29/2016

www.trafford.com

North America & international
toll-free: 1 888 232 4444 (USA & Canada)
fax: 812 355 4082

CONTENTS

Dedicated to all of the brave men and women who served. You are NEVER FORGOTTEN!

FOREWORD

May 7, 1975 marked the end of the Vietnam War and the beginning of the personal war that each Vietnam Veteran would battle in some way, shape or form!

Never Forgotten, by Jenny La Sala is a compilation of personal recollections, of a select group of contributing Vietnam Veterans remembering their service, their sacrifice, and their personal struggles adapting to their lives after combat. Adding insult to their already wounded souls was the heinous treatment and rejection they received from their own country when they returned home. "WELCOME HOME" and "THANKS" was never uttered to these exhausted combat warriors.

There are many Vietnam Veterans today who suffer silently from survivor's guilt and the trauma of haunting, combat flashbacks. The realization of this agonizing plight for so many Nam Vets became the impetus for Jenny La Sala's book, *Never Forgotten.* It is her desire to bridge the gap for these unsung Heroes and bring healing, hope, and closure for their tormented and wounded souls.

The great sacrifices of these service men and women will be evidenced as you read their personal stories. May we develop a deeper sense of empathy and a more compassionate understanding of their lives then and now, as we begin to grasp the impact of their personal battles they have daily struggled with to endure life.

In this world of give and take there are not enough people willing to give what it takes.

Thanks to every Vietnam Veteran for 'Giving What it Takes'.... and 'Welcome Home' to the USA.

~ Patrick Cleburne McClary
United States Marine Corps / 1st Lieutenenant, Retired,
Vietnam Veteran and Motivational Speaker.

INTRODUCTION

"Most soldiers who have witnessed atrocities of war rarely cry except when seeing friends with whom they fought..."
~ Sir Christopher Lee, Actor and WWII Veteran

My ancestors fought in the Civil War and my father was a decorated 101st Airborne paratrooper during WWII. I am the sister of a Gulf War Veteran and I am a former spouse of a Vietnam Veteran.

After the passing of my father and publishing his wartime letters in *Comes A Soldier's Whisper*, I came to fully appreciate, both his greatness and the silent struggles he constantly battled. His letters have allowed me to offer a greater love and compassion to others impacted by what we now know as Post Traumatic Stress Disorder, or PTSD. This silent weapon had a profound effect on my family. It was almost as though my father was ashamed to speak of those horrors of war and through his silence was bound together with his comrades. There were several occasions where my father threatened suicide. It was during the late fifties and early sixties that I remember this quite clearly. Dad would grab his hunting rifle and leave the house, taking off for the woods. I do not believe that he understood that he was suffering from Post Traumatic Stress and post war anger. Perhaps he was instinctively trying to rid himself of his demons. As a young girl, I didn't understand it. Maybe the thing that saved him, was the peace and serenity of nature that he loved so much. I recall the house becoming very quiet and never knowing if he would return. He always did though, and with everyone behaving as though nothing had happened. So this became the 'norm' for my family. It took me over fifty years to come to terms with my father's threats. At first, I did not want to mention it, for fear of dishonoring his memory. But then I realized that my silence was part of the problem, and so I decided to break free from the fear and allow the healing to begin. With the ever-growing rate of suicide among the military and Veterans, my father's behavior was not so very different from the soldiers of today. May we open our hearts so they can take the risk to speak out, heal from it and move forward.

Never Forgotten is the result of collecting hundreds of stories from Veterans of all wars ranging from WWII to what is currently called the War on Terrorism. It is interesting that our country chooses to not call any of the wars since Vietnam, an actual war. They are carefully referred to as a 'conflict' and 'operation'. Perhaps this is a way to avoid protests by the general public like they did during the Vietnam War and yet some of these conflicts and operations have been going on for over twenty years now.

Many, if not all of the people from my generation were involved with the Vietnam War one way or another. I remember the young men in my graduating class of 1969 being drafted and sent to a country so far away. I felt helpless and confused. I have often wondered what happened to those young men from my hometown of Portage, Indiana.

With 2015 marking the 50th Anniversary of the start of the Vietnam War, I felt it appropriate to publish a collection of stories as told by the Vietnam Veteran in his or her own words. It has been an honor and privilege to collect these stories revealing the many layers of the soldier's experience and sacrifice. They are compelling and heartfelt. They reveal a longing for their voices to be heard. Veterans are among the most humble group of Americans that I have ever encountered. If you are looking for a historical and academic resource for the Vietnam War, this book is not for you. The sole purpose of this publication was to 'Welcome Home', our Vietnam Veterans and to share their heartfelt recollections of war. I reached out to them for their stories, many of which declined at first. They were fearful of how they would be perceived. They are still suffering from public opinion of the Vietnam Era, which delayed any chance for rehabilitation. For the most part, Vietnam Veterans did not begin to seek help for PTSD until 35 plus years later and are now in their sixties and seventies, many of whom are experiencing the symptoms of Agent Orange.

The outcome of sharing their stories has been a healing experience for the Veterans in this book, their families and for myself. I feel blessed and honored to have met such a remarkable group of Americans. We should not be ashamed of those things we privately fear, for they never go away. By keeping things bottled up inside, they only get stronger and more powerful. The stories reflect sacrifice and feelings of loneliness, homesickness, and fear by the men and women who served their country in one of the darkest periods of our history. They give insight to what they carried with them on and off the battlefield and still do, to this day.

My mission in life is Veteran advocacy; to share our Veteran's stories one day at a time, and give voice to their silent hearts. It has been both, an emotional and amazing journey to unlock so many unheard voices. This book and the stories in it, will help our present and future generations, learn about war, and the men and women who fought in it. The men and women returning from war have a huge impact on all of our lives. Perhaps in understanding our Veterans and the battles they have endured, we can begin to know ourselves a little bit more.

I have included sentiments from the American people that reflect their support, gratitude, and love for these brave men and women. You will find these sentiments interlaced between each of the stories throughout this book. These were posted comments on my Facebook page, 'Comes A Soldier's Whisper'.

Our nation is a much more caring and appreciative country 50 years after the Vietnam War. I hope that we have learned a valuable lesson in the process; It is okay to hate the war, but not hate the soldier. I believe patriotism is stronger than ever in the United States today.

There are growing numbers of groups who are helping with post-traumatic stress disorder. I hope that we can break down the <u>dis</u>order and bring order to our lives. We need to do this for the soldiers, their families, ourselves, and for America.

When the Vietnam Veteran's tours were over, they came home to find a country divided and a nation unappreciative of their service. How they were treated, how they integrated back into society, and how their wartime experiences changed them are just some of the questions answered, as their stories unfold.

Told by the Veterans themselves, these are their stories.

~ Jenny La Sala

WE HAD A DREAM OF WAR

Waking up to the pale morning sky,
We had a dream of war.
Many died and blood was drawn,
With an unsightly gore.

Our minds were numb,
But still we come,
Stealing the lives of men.
Yes we know it's a sin,
But here we go again.
Wearing heavy combat costs,
Having sleepless nights,
Chasing fear and chasing loss,
Oh what an awful sight.
Our lives have become a battlefi eld,
Forever fighting for our lives,
Many heroes have passed,
Lost in this battle of strife.

We pray for strength and courage,
And hearts that will forgive.
For peace and understanding,
In a world for all to live.

- A Vietnam Veteran

Image By: (GOLD Heart) Michael Hivnor

ROBIN M. CATHCART

U.S. AIR FORCE

"WHEN THE DRAFT ENDED, SO DID THE PROTESTS."

My name is Robin M. Cathcart, and I am a Vietnam Veteran.

Several members of my family served in the military with an uncle serving in a US Army Machine Gun Battalion in France during WW I and another uncle serving as a US Army Infantryman in the Pacific Theater in WW II. My eldest half-brother served as WW II US Army Air Forces Technical Sergeant

(E-6). He was rated an Aerial Gunner on a Boeing B-17G Flying Fortress heavy bomber. My other half-brother, a Chief Petty Officer (E-7), was a rated-Naval Air crewman. He served three cruises. The first was off "Yankee Station" with VA-113, a Douglas A-4D Skyhawk bomber Squadron. The second was off the USS KITTY HAWK (CV-63), and later the third was off the USS ENTERPRISE (CVN-65). "Yankee Station" was with waters off North Vietnam. Aircraft from these carriers launched against the North, while aircraft from carriers off "Dixie Station" launched against targets in South Vietnam. My family never spoke of their wartime experiences.

I was a Cadet Lieutenant Colonel and Cadet Group Commander of Buffalo Group, New York Wing, Civil Air Patrol, and was enlisted in the US Air Force on 10 July 1969. I attended USAF Basic Training at Lackland AFB, near San Antonio, Texas. My first operational assignment was with the 320th Security Police Squadron, Mather AFB, near Sacramento, California. Our mission was to guard nuclear-armed Boeing B-52 Stratofortress bombers on alert duty with a war mission. I volunteered for service in the Republic of Vietnam immediately after arriving at Mather AFB.

I was assigned to the 35th Security Police Squadron at Phan Rang Airbase, Republic of Vietnam, and departed for RVN on 1 May 1970, the day of the "Kent State Massacre." For the first three months of my tour I spent about five days a week manning a machine gun tower on the perimeter of the airbase and one day a week riding vehicle patrol in an M151A1 jeep, mounting a 7.62mm machine gun. We also carried two M-16 rifles, one with a grenade launching attachment, and two .38 caliber revolvers.

Following a 30-day emergency leave, I returned to my squadron. We had a new First Sergeant. He learned that I had been nominated three times for appointment to the US Air Force Academy and once for West Point. The First Sergeant decided that I ought to work as a clerk in the Orderly Room. I had taken typing in high school so that gave me "added appeal" in his eyes. The worst part of my service occurred when I was rejected and constantly harassed and insulted by my fellow first-term security policemen. I wanted to make the military my career.

I developed heart disease due to exposure to herbicides in Vietnam and had a bad experience when dealing with the Veterans Administration. When a VA employee saw that I served in Vietnam, he said, "Humpf! I am a World War II Veteran. We won our war!" I later decided to avoid dealing with the VA for 30 years, and lost thousands of dollars in VA disability compensation.

Some of the men who protested directly against the war were committed to ending the war, but participating in war protests was a great way for a young man to meet young women. When the draft came to an end and college students knew they could avoid military service, the protests came to an end too. Some of these men were just cowards!

To find out what happened after the war, just talk to a Vietnamese-American who lived through it. It meant Death for all RVN General officers, and jail time for all other military officers. It also meant that professional men who supported the RVN were forbidden from practicing their professions.

~ Robin M. Cathcart, USAF, Vietnam Veteran

> **"**
>   When I arrived back in the world from Nam, my greeting from family members was total silence.
>
> That was the first feeling of rejection and one of many that would follow.
> **"**
>
> ~ Vietnam Vet

Thomas B. Daly

U.S. Army

"Find the bastards and then pile on."

I enlisted March 16, 1966 because I ran out of options in civilian life and believed in the American way.

Initially, I was sent to Fort Gordon, Georgia for basic training and then to Fort Jackson, South Carolina for advanced individual training (AIT), where I became a heavy-wheeled vehicle operator.

Although I volunteered to go to Vietnam, I was sent to Germany until I turned 18 when I could go to Vietnam.

During my service in Germany as a Spec 4 with a mechanized infantry battalion, in my unusually, loosely supervised position, I was able to train in different infantry tasks and learn the way of Army organization and operations, which would later serve me well in the Republic of Vietnam. After volunteering again at age 18 and receiving orders to deploy to Vietnam, I was assigned as a Sgt. to Car Airborne Company of the II Field Forces, as a driver for senior officers and civilian staff members. After becoming disillusioned in a protected position, I again volunteered to serve with the 11th Armored Cavalry Regiment; A well-known fighting unit commanded by Col. George Patton, Jr. This was a separate, mobile crisis-responding unit, assigned to the II Field Forces whose motto was "Find the bastards and then pile on." A prime example of this was the TET Offensive of 1968, when I was assigned to 1st squadron, 11th Armored Cavalry Regiment (1/11th Cav). I soon acknowledged what war was all about and how difficult it was. My service in the 11th brought me to areas in and around Loc Ninh, An Loc, Lai Khe and Xuan Loc, among other vacation spots in the Republic of Vietnam.

Serving as the truck master for the 1/11, I established relationships with some of the greatest people I have ever met. Their dedication to each other and to duty, led me to some of the strongest bonds in my entire life. My worst memory was of a Vietnamese worker's school bus, which hit a land mine resulting in many, many casualties.

Shown in this picture taken in Vietnam is Spec 4 Zimmerman, the only man that I am aware of whose truck was heavily damaged by a land mine, and apologized for its demise afterwards.

The ambush patrols along with the fear and realization of my comrades being wounded or worse, was a constant reality, which sometimes came through with dire results. These are experiences one does not forget. The 11th Cav or ACR my unit worked with was the Big Red One, 1st Infantry Division. I continuously worked throughout the time I was with the CAV in a supporting role. The Cav added intense firepower with heavily armored fighting vehicles to the 1st Infantry Division. These supporting operations were mostly conducted just north of Saigon to the Cambodian Border, adjacent to Highway 13, otherwise known as "Thunder Road". These were not especially nice places to visit but war is what we all make it! Anyone who fired rounds or was fired upon has some sort of hearing loss. My hearing loss was due to high frequencies caused by firing 50 caliber machine guns both in and out of actual combat. There are certain speech levels and crowd background noises that impede my hearing. Subconsciously, to make up for my loss, I automatically smile and save the embarrassment of asking over and over what was said. This tactic seems to please the recipients more often than not and saves me from not so enjoyable outcomes. All types of explosions happened around me throughout my military career, from tank fire to mortar fire, and even explosives that I set up. The actual hostile mortar or rocket fire was never close enough to cause any damage, or more than likely I would be dead.

My wartime experiences were later reflected in my life as learning points and understandings of the world we live in. The good memories for me were my association with the lowest ranking soldiers, having been one, and how directives and orders affected them. I always made sure that things were fair and logical to them.

My family was happy to see me come home. But as experienced by many other Vietnam Vets, there was no open recognition of the tasks performed. The protestors at the time, I did not feel were appropriate. But in retrospect, if their true challenge were to stop the war, they would have been correct. I do believe that everyone should have a responsibility to the country with some form of national service, to which our future leaders would become well versed in our world realities.

I spent the next ten years as a civilian working as a lineman, police officer, and fire fighter, but never ever a cowboy. I was a Sergeant when I was in Vietnam. Ten years after my Vietnam experience, I went through officer's candidate school, retiring as a Major with 24 years of service in the U.S. Army, Ret. Corps of Engineers. This photo is with a Captain in the passenger seat during an observing, engineer operation. At the time I was a

Company Commander. The last two photos were taken later in my military career in CONUS, (contiguous US).

Today, I am happily retired, working on a soon-to-be horse farm in Central North Carolina.

~ Major Thomas B. Daly, (U.S. Army Ret.) Corps of Engineers, Vietnam Veteran

> **"**
> It makes me so happy to see Vets helping Vets. We are the only ones who really understand what it was like at war and therefore we are the best support system for each other.
> **"**
>
> ~ Nam Vet

JOHN C. WOLF

U.S. ARMY

"IT IS NOW MY MISSION IN LIFE."

My name is John C Wolf, II. My friends call me "Wolfie."

I served in the Army, with Delta Company 1st of the 20th Infantry, 11th Light Infantry Brigade, 23rd Infantry Division after being drafted and inducted on May 5, 1970.

I drew # 30 in the lottery and went to the Los Angeles induction center with X-rays and a letter from my orthopedic surgeon saying I was 4-F. I almost killed myself on a motorcycle accident the year before, breaking my left femur, which needed major surgery. I had an 18", 9mm steel shaft inserted into the middle of my femur. I was inducted because I was told that I 'fogged the mirror when I breathed on it'.

I was a grunt, received the Combat Infantry Badge, Bronze Star, Air Medal and all the other normal medals for serving in Vietnam with Good Conduct. I was promoted to Sergeant, but they told me I would have to sign up for 4 more years to officially become one. During Nam I was a rifleman, walked point, carried an M203 (M16 and M79 grenade launcher over and under) and then became squad, platoon and company RTO (Radio-Telephone Operator). In some ways I ran our company because all communications went through me. One of our CO's (commanding officers), was a bad officer and didn't like to talk on the radio. He was later relieved for cowardice in the face of the enemy. I had to 'call in' and manage the jets, artillery, gunships and Dustoffs (casualty evacuations from a combat zone).

Some of my relatives fought as Indians in the Indian Wars in the 1870's, but not in the U.S. Army, because they were on the other side. I am certified by the Bureau of Land Management as a Choctaw Indian and get the monthly newspaper, birthday and Xmas gifts every year.

One of the worst experiences I had was after being in the field for only about 4 weeks. A new buddy of mine was walking in front of me and tripped a booby trap. He and the guy in front of him took most of the blast. His nickname was Zombie. The explosion knocked me down too. Once I got up, I ran over to him and checked his wounds. I immediately put some plastic over his chest wound and then gave him CPR for the next 20 plus minutes until the Dustoff bird arrived. I will never forget looking at his face. I carried Zombie to the chopper and later learned he and the other guy died. To this day, I feel guilty. A great guy died, and I, who was only a few feet away, lived. He was called Zombie because he liked the C-ration fruitcake. It was awful. Everyone always gave him the fruitcake and that's how he became known affectionately as Zombie. Only days after I got into the field for the first time, it was monsoon season and we couldn't get resupplied. We were starving. Zombie pulled out his fruitcake and gave it to us and saved the day.

The wartime experience has changed me. After serving in the infantry, carrying up to 85 pounds on my back at times, humping the bush for weeks, and jumping out of helicopters, I have a bad back. The VA told me having one leg shorter than the other was due to my accident and that doing the above had no direct cause to my back problems over the years.

My greatest fear was getting my legs blown off. I was flown to my unit via a hospital helicopter that landed at the emergency area with supplies. I was told to wait in a room until another bird could take me to where my unit was. I was in the entry to the

ER, sitting there for about 10 minutes when a helicopter landed. They wheeled a guy in, who had his legs blown off below the knees. That was my first introduction to combat.

I started suffering from PTSD sometime in the late 80's, but blocked it out until I retired in 2009. It has gotten progressively worse. I suffer from nightmares from the event with Zombie and the Easter Sunday ambush in 1971. Eleven men were killed in an ambush including the Chaplain, who had come out to give us Easter Services and Communion. It was the 4th, worst, single casualty battle in 1971. For what it's worth, the Veterans Administration has turned me down for PTSD (Post Traumatic Stress Disorder) compensation; I didn't fight it the first time. Even though the VA treats me for PTSD, and has issued 4 prescribed medications, the VA compensation board says there is no proof that my military experiences caused my PTSD. I have submitted an FOIA request for all information related to their denial decision and am providing, it to an attorney that has taken on my case.

I flew from Vietnam into Ft. Lewis Washington, and connected in San Francisco before flying to Los Angeles near my home. While I walked to the gate for the LA flight, a hippie seeing my combat fatigues came up and spit on me. He called me a baby killer. That's when saying you were a Vietnam Veteran was not well advised. When I came back from Nam, I tried to block it out. I put my movies and pictures into a closet; For what I thought was forever.

In 2005 my wife and I decided to go to the traveling Vietnam Memorial Wall that had come to our town. We returned around 4:30 p.m. on a Saturday and at 4:30 a.m. the next morning, my wife came into my office and asked why I had not been to bed. I told her I had been in technology for 25 years and had never 'Googled' anything about Vietnam. During those 12 hours researching on line that night, I found my unit and was able to find buddies I served with. One of them asked if I still had the movies I took. I wasn't sure, but found out my dad had taken the 8mm film and had it converted to VHS. I had never viewed that tape, but found it and watched it for the first time. I then decided to take the footage and make a tribute to the 11 that died on Easter Sunday. After posting the first video to You Tube in 2007 my life changed.

Most of the military people involved in the Easter Sunday ambush have contacted me after they or their friends found my videos on

You Tube. The pilot of the Chaplain's helicopter that was shot down sat in my living room just 6 days later, after he found my video on line. The families and friends of those killed on Easter Sunday found their loved ones names on my tribute video and have contacted me wanting to know more about their loved ones passing. The Army never told them how these men died, only that they died in combat. This led to some pretty emotional calls. I felt it was my duty to try and help bring some closure to them.

I was able to block out most of my bad Vietnam experiences until around 2007, when I got reconnected with a former CO (commanding officer) of my unit. He had gone to the National Archives and got all the Daily After Action Reports. These reports were sent every day from each company to Battalion and they gave map coordinates, the names of those hurt or killed and any other things that happened. This refreshed my memory and gave me info I was not aware of.

As I look back on it, reconnecting with old buddies brought back some terrible memories, but that is now history. I wanted to help my Vietnam buddies get out of their caves not realizing how it might later effect me later on. Because of my videos there have been countless times I have gotten buddies back together.

I have become dedicated to helping vets get back together and bring honor to them. I am part of several Vietnam related groups on Face Book and am working on a charity related website (http://www.22muststop.org). This site is dedicated to stopping or reducing the 22 plus vets and current military who commit suicide each day. This is high number is unacceptable. We must get more recognition and stop the insanity.

It is now my mission in life.

~ John C. Wolf, U.S. Army, Vietnam Veteran

"
We have shared the incommunicable experience of war, we have felt, we still feel, the passion of life to its top. In our youth- our hearts were touched with fire.
"

~ Oliver Wendell Holmes

TOM BATCHELOR

U.S. ARMY

"THERE WERE SO MANY UNITS AND LOCATIONS. WE WERE ALL THERE AT THE SAME TIME."

My dad, my older brother and I were in Vietnam in 1968, all there in the same unit in Special Forces.

I was mostly II and III Corps the first year with the 101st Airborne home base in Tuy Hoa and later with the 5th Special Forces in Nha Trang and then to Kontum. We were all assigned to the 5th Special Forces but were in different camps. Even though the camps were close to each other, we did not interact with each other. I believe that anyone who served in the military changes in some way or another for the good or for the bad. Each person changes in his own way. As for being in combat, you grow up real fast or you don't make it. Mostly, my mind matured very much. I became aware of life and living. I have always wondered how one makes it through all those firefights while others do not. I spent three tours in Vietnam. I was always on the ground and only slightly wounded once. I attended countless funerals. I will never understand why someone else died and I didn't. Like anyone else who was there, I have good and bad memories.

Dad served in WWII, Korea, and Vietnam with 36 years of service. He started his service in August 1936 and went to jump school in 1942, serving with the 11th ABN Division during WWII. He retired in September 1972. The group picture in military uniform is my dad, my two brothers, my younger sister and myself. My older brother did 26 years, mostly with Special Forces with two tours in Nam. My young sister, Diana Batchelor did 22 years in the Air Force retiring as an LTC (Lieutenant Colonel). Our younger brother did 26 years and several trips to Afghanistan and Iraq. My oldest son has completed 5 years with two trips to Afghanistan. He was badly hurt and has medically retired. My youngest son has completed 10 years and is still on active duty.

I did 25 years in U.S. Army from August 1964 to November 1989, mostly with Special Forces. I spent a little time in the 82nd Airborne Division and a year with the 101st Airborne in Vietnam. I completed three tours in Nam. The group of soldiers was taken in 1969, Nha Tranke Mike Force. Left to right is Sam Huggins, myself, Walt Hetzler and Manuel Gonzales.

I graduated from AIT as an 11C, Mortars, and went to SF school as a Weapons Specialist. Later in my career, I went to SCUBA school and became a Dive Supervisor. I also went to HALO school, became a HALO Free-Fall Jumpmaster, and spent two years as Drill Sgt, at Ft Jackson, SC.

We have about 10,000 members in the Special Forces Association. Each year in June, we have a convention at a different location in the USA. The next one in 2016 will be in Fayetteville, North Carolina, home of the Special Forces. The average number of people that attend is about 1,500. However, we have about 2,500 in Fayetteville and expect a large attendance.

There are presently over 100 chapters around the world and that is how we keep in touch with our Special Forces Brothers.

~ Tom Batchelor, U.S. Army, Special Forces, Vietnam Veteran

> **"**
> I had a cousin that flew Nam. He served 3 tours. He was a medivac pilot and said on most occasions he was taking heavy enemy fire while trying to load the wounded.
> **"**
>
> ~ Patriot

MICHAEL DALE LANE

U.S. ARMY

"I CONSIDER MYSELF LUCKY TO BE LIVING EVERYDAY PAST VIETNAM."

In 1966 at the age of 21, I was drafted by the United States Army to fight, serve, and protect our country.

I left behind my new career, my life, my wife, friends and family. I did what I was told to do. I attended boot camp in Fort Lewis, Washington and went to Advanced Individual Training (AIT) at the United States 6th Army headquarters in Presidio of San

Francisco and was finally sent to Cam Ranh Bay, Vietnam to fight in the Vietnam War as a Sergeant E-5. I was actively part of the Military Assistance Command, Vietnam (MACV), the United States Army Republic of Vietnam (USARV), and the TET Offensive, fighting for our freedom until November 19, 1968. It was time to go back home with an honorable discharge and medals including Republic of Vietnam Campaign Medal; Vietnam Service Medal with 2 Bronze Service Stars; Sharpshooter (Rifle); and the National Defense Service Medal.

I'm the first man of our immediate family to serve in the war or in any type of war. I did not have any knowledge of war or how the war would be until I was actually in the midst of the war itself. Unfortunately, none of us had a chance to imagine anything or to think twice, because the first thing that was expected of us was to fight. You were either going to make it or not. There is a lot to be afraid of, but not knowing what to expect out of being drafted into the war, not having any knowledge of what to expect from war has been one of my greatest fears. It was the not knowing what was going to happen next that was hard. I didn't know if tomorrow was going to become today, or if I was going to survive, or if I was going to receive a "Dear John" letter.

The mortar attacks were common. The base camp that I was stationed in was one of the safer spots before the TET Offensive. We had green, orange, and red alerts. Red meant we were under attack. It was my turn to go on the 2400-1200 night shift, which happened to be the night that we got over-run and put on RED alert. My job was to destroy documents and to protect the large metal shipping container called CONEX.

Since most of the fighting was done during nighttime, we could not see. I was not able to destroy many documents because I was focused on protecting the CONEX. That night the door swung open suddenly. I could not see and, yelled, "HALT! Who is there?" I didn't get a response. I had a 45 caliber on me and I pulled it out of my holster asking one more time, "Who is it?" Once again, nobody answered. For some reason, something was telling me not to fire, so I didn't fire. It was one of our Colonels drunk off his ass. I told him: "SIR! I almost KILLED you." He came to let me know I was needed in the weapons room because it was my turn to be on the line. As we went there together, I got him help, and waited for further orders from there.

All I could hear were screams, gunfire, and mortars. I heard people fighting for their lives. It was finally my turn to fight so I took my position on the line at the perimeter. Sometimes we were in the holes in the ground and other times we were flat on the ground. When I was in the line was when I was the most scared. In my mind I was just so really scared. All I wanted to do was run but there was no place to run to because the whole country was under siege. The scared part never leaves me. Those are the nightmares that I have always had and always will have for the rest of my life. We were on RED alert for two weeks. If the fire I threw down killed anybody, I don't want to know. In my heart I know what I have done and did. We were trained to kill. When you come back to life without war, you always have to live with your actions during war. We have to live with it for the rest of our lives.

On November 19, 1968 after being discharged from the U.S. Army and arriving in Fort Hood, Texas, I never expected to see the general population protesting against the War that I had just sacrificed myself for. I was more than proud to wear the uniform because I loved my country. Everything that I had envisioned as a young man ended up changing my perspective on life. Everything was changed because of the war. War changed everything. It didn't take long to realize that the soldiers coming home weren't being treated right. Soon, we were told to strip out of our uniforms, for safety of course. However, even being out of uniform, people could still recognize us compared to other men, just by the way that we carried ourselves. After all, we were soldiers.

Some places that I visited, including simple little restaurants, would refuse to serve me because they were against the soldiers and the Vietnam War. Being young and naive, I never thought in a million years that people would be this way. I was very surprised and hurt that they had the kind of heart to treat a man and soldier with such disrespect. Confused and broken, all I wanted to know was why people were protesting. We went to war because we loved our country thinking we were fighting for our families, and for our freedom. It only took a short time being in the military to catch a grasp on the concept that the government really didn't care about our young men. We were nothing more than a number.

Being a strong believer and a believer in fate, I always felt that my number wasn't up. The other men and I that made it back home felt bad for the men that didn't make it home, and especially for their families. But I was still proud to come back home. In some ways, I am still at war and suffering from Post Traumatic Stress, every second, every moment and every hour of each day.

I know that any man that has gone to war and comes back the same, if they do come back the same, is one hell of a man! I also suffered from jungle rot and recurrent malaria. PTSD was and is very common upon returning to civilian life. The hardest part about it back then was not having any help. The most difficult and frustrating part of my readjustment was the fact that I tried to reach out for help and didn't get it. Because PTSD wasn't acknowledged until 1980, I didn't receive any help for it. All I wanted was help in trying to get my somewhat, normal civilian life back. All I wanted were the night sweats, the loud noises, and the nightmares, to settle down.

Today I also suffer from Agent Orange-a herbicide and defoliant used by the U.S. Military. Recently I discovered that my CHF disease (Chronic Heart Failure), and heart attack of a main artery, which resulted in open-heart surgery, is linked directly back to Agent Orange. Throughout my whole life, I have been suffering with things that I never realized were from the war. I'm dying from this disease, but I consider myself lucky to be living everyday past Vietnam. Suffering from PTSD and Agent Orange, I still find time to be happy and grateful. I have a family that respects and honors the fact that I served our country.

I never realized how having served would ultimately affect my daughter. Being the child of a Vietnam Veteran has taken its toll. My daughter became very curious about my service and as a school project, she chose the topic of the 'Vietnam War'. She asked me to come to her class and speak about the war. I didn't know that I would get choked up and tear up while talking. My daughter could see my pain and she has been hungry to learn more ever since my talk. If your children and grandchildren ask about your wartime experiences, sit down and talk with them. You'll be glad you did.

The 'Vietnam Veterans Memorial Wall' inscribes how many men we lost in Vietnam, but we're still losing Vietnam Veterans every day, and will continue every day until the last soldier is gone.

-Michael Dale Lane, U.S. Army, Vietnam Veteran

"
Some scars never heal.

They get a little more tolerant with time but never go away because you can't un-see events you have seen.

They play in your mind like a tape recorder.
"

~ Vietnam Vet

GERALD JOSEPH PELLETIER

U.S. ARMY

"THE WORST PART WAS WITNESSING MY FELLOW SOLDIERS DIE OR SUFFER."

My name is Gerald Joseph Pelletier.

I was drafted on October 1, 1965 and served with the U.S. Army from October 1965 and July 1967 with the 196th Light Infantry Brigade and 82nd Artillery, A Battery. In country I was assigned to 2/1 Inf of 196 LIB.

My grandfather served in WWI and my dad served on the LCT 590, which landed prior to the first wave of men at Omaha Beach during WWII. The story of trying to land tanks on Omaha Beach and the failure of the operation can be found in the book, *Omaha Beach, D-Day* by Joseph Baloski.

The one time my Dad did talk about D-Day was when we were all visiting the D-Day Memorial in Bedford, Virginia. As we were walking through, we could all see what happened to his ship and friends, was too painful for him to talk about. I had two uncles who served in WWII. Uncle Jerry KIA at the Battle of the Bulge and died April 1945. I was born three months later, and named after him. Another Uncle served in Korea and I served in Vietnam.

I can remember two distinct conversations with my dad before I was sworn in. He told me to listen to what I was told to do, do

what I was told, and stay under the radar and never volunteer for anything. Before leaving for Vietnam, he told me to take the top bunk in the troop carrier so other Soldiers would not throw up on me, be careful and to come back to them.

As a Forward Observer I was responsible for directing fire for close air support in situations using helicopters, and artillery. I directed fire into places where the enemy was positioned, while I supported troops on the ground. A Forward observer team includes a person who carries the radio and a second person who calls in the coordinates for a fire mission. Because artillery is an indirect, fire weapon system, the guns are never in the line of sight of their target and are located tens of miles away.

Other positions were considered high priority targets by enemy forces, as they controlled a great amount of firepower and were within visual range of the enemy. As part of the FO team we were often located deep within enemy territory. The worst part for me was witnessing my fellow Soldiers die or suffer such horrific injuries in the jungle, many of whom were my friends. To

this day, I can close my eyes and still see and hear cries of pain and fear from the men, as a result of their gruesome injuries, as they screamed, "Am I going to die?" and "Please, please save me, I do not want to die."

My greatest fear while in Nam was getting captured or ending up blind from injuries. I returned from Nam in July 1967. The reception was very negative at the San Francisco Airport. I began college in August 1967. When students and teachers found out I was a Vietnam Vet many confronted me as if I was the enemy and not someone who was drafted and served in the military. They had their minds made up that our participation in Vietnam was wrong and all of us who were there were bad guys. Here I was someone who had spent 12 months fighting with the South Vietnamese people and against the VC and NVRA and I could not come to a conclusion that our involvement was good or bad. It was difficult to understand how others could view me as a "killer" and be so sure their convictions were right when they had never been to Vietnam to see what was really going on.

One of the re-adjustments I had to make when I returned home was to lose my habit of swearing. In Nam we swore constantly and I do remember having the problem of trying to get rid of that habit. There was no time to adjust from fighting in the jungles one day to a week later, walking the streets in your hometown.

Whenever I am experiencing a bad day or event, I compare it to being in the jungles with what I am experiencing at the time, including when I lost my job. The comparison always brought everything into perspective.

My Vietnam War experience changed my life both physically and emotionally. Because of my exposure to Agent Orange, I suffer from Peripheral Neuropathy, which limits my ability to walk. I had a radical prostatectomy due to prostate cancer leaving me with many side effects including irreversible Erectile Dysfunction, Gastroesophageal Reflux surgery and Barrett's. I have PTSD, tremors, anxiety, depression, anger issues, irritability, loneliness, and want to avoid crowds. Most of all, I have the fear of the unknown.

Fortunately I was able to fight through my demons and manage a good career in broadcasting including 30 years of management experience and owning my own business. I was on both the ABC and CBS affiliate boards and worked with collegiate conferences such as the ACC, SEC, Big10, Big 8, Pac 10, NCAA Men, Women's Basketball Final Four and national events. I also worked with the CBS/US Olympic Committee, Davis Cup and the Men and Women's Professional Tennis Organizations.

Today I am retired and spend time with my four grandchildren who are the love of my life.

~ Gerald Joseph Pelletier, U.S. Army, Vietnam Veteran

" I had many friends die in Vietnam.

I was a protestor during the Vietnam War because I was tired of watching my friends come home in coffins or wounded in body and mind. No one could give me a good reason Americans were sacrificing our young men in Vietnam. I never have given our military anything but the highest respect. I never protested against the military, but I did protest our involvement in the war.

Though I proudly remain a hippie, I have worked hard for Veteran's rights, volunteered at the USO and in Veteran's homes. **"**

~ Patriot

CHARLES LEONARD TRYON

U.S. NAVY

"MY MISSION WAS TO CAPTURE IT ON FILM."

I was born in Troy, New York, August 1945.

One of my hobbies was photography, which I learned from a former WWII Marine combat photographer in 1960. I worked with him to earn money to attend college. My other interest was scuba diving.

Several of my family members served in the military. My Uncle Charles, who lived next door to us, became a mail clerk after he was in the Army during WWII. My Uncle Leonard was KIA in the Battle of the Bulge in 1944. Dad shared some stories that were written by Uncle Leonard's battle buddies on how he died. A sniper killed him. I wish I had met him.

I was attending college in 1968 when drafting for Vietnam started. I had one class to complete before graduating. During this time, I was reclassified from 2-S (student) to a 1-A (eligible for military service). Within a matter of weeks, I was to report to the Army. I wanted to finish college and then enlist with the Navy and become a photographer like my former neighbor and WWII Veteran. I went to the Navy and they were able to give me a deferment to finish school prior to going to boot camp and active duty.

In the fall of 1968, I reported aboard the U.S.S. Newport News, CA-148, a heavy cruiser out of Norfolk, Virginia. The ship was preparing to deploy to West Pack in South East Asia, Vietnam. While onboard ship, I prepared to be a "Striker" and Photographer's Mate, an aviation rate in the Navy. Our first gun line action was December 1968 off of Da Nang. Our ship, the Newport News, was called "Thunder". We provided gunfire support to our Marines on shore and up and down the coast of South Vietnam and the inland waterways.

As a photographer, my job was to record the action as it unfolded day after day during our deployment. I witnessed small craft as well as people and bunkers blow up in real time. Using a telephoto lens I got up front and personal with the action. The job of the ship was to kill and destroy the enemy. My mission was to capture it on film. I watched and waited for the action to take place. I could hear the screams, watch the horror unfold and smell the burning flesh after our shells hit their target. In most cases, the gathering of intelligence and action on film was by nature, 'Top Secret'. I was told many times that I was invisible and did not exist. I could only share my thoughts and experiences with those that worked with me. Keeping things bottled up was a day-to-day activity. There was a great deal of fear when I was capturing the events on film. After all, I was told that I was invisible and due to the sensitive nature of the material on hand, I felt disposable and that no one cared. I worked among other photographers and men who knew that every day could be our last day. We worked as one and watched each other's back. It was survival. This photograph is of me attached to the super structure of the aft section of our ship during 'Flight Operations'. I did this to capture some of the ships activity. Many individuals and materials came aboard using Helo drops.

There is one particular memory that has always stayed with me. Early one morning our ship was called to support some of our Marines. They were located on Monkey Mountain. We came close to the shore area and watched the action unfold with the enemy above, our Marines in the center, and the enemy below. The location was called in and fired upon.

The radio went silent. I was ordered to secure the photo detail. Nothing more was said about that moment. It was quiet. I know what I observed. Our men had come under fire, our own fire. Not a word was said, nor could I ask. I have kept these details in my mind for some 50 years. I met two Marines at a 2014 Veteran's Retreat who were on Monkey Mountain during that moment when our own Marines were hit and injured. They heard my story and came over and said, "Welcome Home." I felt ashamed and guilty. But they said we all had a job to do and did what we were told. From that day so long ago, I was given closure to my thoughts. When the U.S. pulled out of Vietnam, I remember thinking that our job was not done. We could have done more, so our soldiers and Veterans had a purpose for their sacrifices. Americans hated the Veterans of the Vietnam War. As for protestors of that war or any war, they are lucky they can protest and not be killed for it. There are other places in the world where human life means nothing. One of the prices I paid for, is called "Freedom".

I attend Veteran's events and activities in my area to give back some hope to the Veterans of today. Freedom is not free. I honor those who did not come home and cherish their memories. They are the true heroes.

I always wanted to find out why people became bad guys, so I went into police work. After 30 years as a homicide detective, I still don't have the answer.

~ Charles Leonard Tryon, U.S. Navy, Vietnam Veteran

> **"**
> It's good to read these stories because sometimes we think we are all alone back here in the 'world' as we use to say. **"**
>
> ~ Vietnam Vet

KENNY TORNABENE

U.S NAVY

"IT WAS LIKE A FIRE IN OUR CHEST."

As a Vietnam ERA Veteran, I was never 'in country' according to the government.

I served in the Navy and was on a SH-3G Helicopter. I was Photo Recon, Combat Camera Group 2 and was stationed aboard a small carrier. We would fly over and do our thing. I had my camera in hand and a 1911 always on my hip. I was one of the fortunate ones and was never physically hurt, but the photos I took still haunt me and hurt to this day. Many of them were what would be called forensic and/or autopsy records. I still don't know why every dead brother brought aboard was to be photographed. But that was my job. In order to be an 'in country' Vet, you were required to have 24 plus hours on Viet Nam soil. All of the flying over that we conducted didn't matter or count. We did not know this at the time and were just thankful that we always made it back to the ship. Had I known this, I would have done the time and then I would be an 'in country' Vet. This is one of the things that I am still fighting over, along with many other guys. Hopefully the D.O.D. will change this and let those of us have our 'due.'

How lucky I was being the only E-5 certified as aerial and forensic. Later in my career I also picked up underwater and had one of the best tours with Seal Team 2 down in Puerto Rico, Old Rossi Roads NAS FltAvComCen. Those were three great years, and if they had let me, I would still be there. Diving with the Seals and Flying with VC-8 were and still are, some of the best memories I have.

My older brother was a 'three tour,' 'in country' Navy Seal Veteran, and better man than I will ever be. He is now at peace and was buried at sea after serving 32 years and retiring as an E-9, Master Chief. Even though we shared many of the same problems together we never discussed them with each other. I guess we both just knew. I enlisted rather than wait to be drafted into the Army, so the Navy was my choice. I wanted a career and a profession that I could use throughout my life. The profession I got was in Aerial / Underwater and Forensic Photography. I was one of only about 20 in the Navy that had all three. Due to my skills in all 3 things, I was in great demand back then and so I was moved around a lot. I was stationed aboard a small carrier, which only handled SH3G helicopters. It was made by Sikorsky, and very much like a Huey that the Army used. We also did a large amount of Aerial/Photo Recon with many of these photos being used to plan out the strategy for the ground troops.

I was like most guys on my first trip to 'The Wall' and couldn't do the walk. As I turned to leave a young lady asked why I was there. We talked a little and she explained that the dad she never got to meet was on the wall and she had hoped that I would help her find him. For some reason this took all my fears, tears and problems away. I guess we helped each other that day. We found her dad and together as we walked the wall side by side, not really saying much, but yet we knew our thoughts were for each other. Now mind you at that time I was a member of the Viet Nam Vets M.C. and was there with several hundred other brothers, all of us dealing with our own demons. I couldn't understand why there was not one brother to help us in our search. Why her? Why then? And why with me? God truly does work in his own strange ways. I have been back now 5 more times, and each time I do the same thing with another vet having his own problems being there. As I walk with him I tell him about this pretty young lady and how she in her own way was there for me. By the time our talk was over, we had walked the wall. I always leave a veteran with just one request; I ask that he give help to a brother in need, either there or anywhere they should meet.

My daughter and I have been really bonding and discussing my time in the service, and I am very happy, as we really didn't have this relationship before. She has talked a lot with me about my service time and now she seems so open about many of the things I did and went through. We have had our differences, which have been major between us, but time really has cured most of them. She now has a family of her own. She has 3 boys all less than 12 years of age, so she has come a long way. She asked me; "Dad, how did you raise all of us alone with everything on your plate that was going on?" The fact that she now sees the things that were in my mind and life is amazing to me. She wants to know and understand and accept who and what I am. Well, all I can say is thank God for letting me have this. She is my youngest, will always be my baby, and 32 years old. It's so good between us compared to what we used to be like.

I saw on the news about an Army Vet that wrote a children's book about PTSD. The way he described it was 'a fire in his heart'. I've never heard it put that way but it really sums it up in one sentence. "A fire in our chest" works for me and I will use it from now on.

The fire just keeps burning and we can't put it out.

~ Kenny Tornabene, U.S. Navy, Vietnam Era Veteran

"   I was born in 1959 so I grew up with Vietnam in every newscast and adult conversation around me.

You are all Heroes. You were called and you served. You fought a war as hard as any other troop. Perhaps you fought harder than most due to the climate and lack of adequate equipment and munitions.

Surely you should all hold your heads high and know you are the troops I think of when I hear the word HERO!

You fought for all our freedoms, even for those who protested the war.

"

~ Patriot

DAVID SCHOFIELD

U.S. AIR FORCE

"I TOOK THIS COUNTRY FOR GRANTED."

My name is David Schofield, and I am a Proud Vietnam Veteran having served in Cam Ranh Bay, Vietnam with the 39th Air Rescue & Recovery Squadron.

I registered for the draft after High School. My best friend and I enlisted in the Air Force under the buddy system. After our physicals they told my best friend that he had too much sugar in his urine and I told them about my severe migraines headaches as a kid. They said I should check with my doctor. But if my best friend wasn't going then I wasn't. We both got jobs at the same company and worked until the lottery came out in 1970. My number was 126 and my best friend's was 300 something. My boss at my company was a Lt. Colonel in the National Guard. I was scheduled for a physical to go into the National Guard

because I did not want to go to Nam. On Memorial Day weekend my mother opened up a letter to me from Uncle Sam, which said "Greetings". I took it to my boss and he called his Captain who said there was nothing they could do since it had been opened. That is when I ran to the Air Force recruiter and showed him the draft notice and said I didn't want to go in the Army. He said that would be fine and I could go into the Air Force.

I was in the Air Force from June 1970 to October 1976 and received orders for Vietnam right out of technical school. I took a special class at Travis AFB and then went to Cam Ranh Bay, Vietnam with an assignment to the 39th ARRS as a 2nd assisted crew chief. The planes were C-130 refuelers. The job of our planes was to be at the Command Center for Jolly Greens trying to extract someone, along with refueling the Jolly Greens. As time went on and people rotated, I got my Sergeant stripes and became a crew chief. I served in Vietnam from January 1971 to the end of March 1972, and from there I was stationed at Eglin AFB, Field 9 834 Field Maintenance Sq (TAC). In June of 1973 I reenlisted and left shortly thereafter. I was stationed at Langley AFB to be closer to home in Baltimore, Maryland where I was attached to the 316th OMS.

I was an Aircraft Maintenance Specialist (crew chief) for C-130 Hercules aircraft for the first 4 years of my Air Force service. In 1974, after coming back from temporary duty in England I received orders to be stationed at Hickam AFB, with the 6594 test group to be a flight crewmember. First I had to attend Water Survival School in Florida and Jungle Survival School at Fairchild AFB, Washington. After completing survival school, they put me back on the flight line as a crew chief again.

My uncle served in the Air Force in the early 60's as an Intelligence Specialist. He served in the states and overseas, but never in a war zone. My brother joined the Air Force after graduation with his best friend. He was an Ejection Seat Specialist serving at Dover AFB, in Korat, Thailand, and Luke AFB in Arizona. Then I did another tour in Ubon, Thailand. My brother talked very little about his tours in Thailand or his temporary time in Vietnam.

Cam Ranh Bay was the largest base in Vietnam. It was an R&R site for the guys to get away from the war for a couple weeks. My squadron barracks was 5 miles from the base on a hill we called Herky. Charlie blew up the ammo dump more the 5 miles away but it still knocked guys out of their bunks. It was a nice show from where we were. They blew up the fuel dump, which was another good show. The scariest part for me was when I was watching a movie at the outdoor theater, at the terminal, and Charlie lobbed in some mortar rounds. We had to scramble for cover wherever we could find it. We had to stay under cover until we got the 'all clear.'

I don't believe my wartime service changed me much. When I first got home I was jumpy when cars or trucks would backfire. We slept in open-air barracks miles away from the main base. We were not allowed to have our weapons, and they were locked up in the First Sergeants Hooch. When I was short they caught Charlie at the base of Herky Hill. If he had gotten through the fence he could have shot us at random.

In Dec 1971 I extended to get a free 30-day leave to come home and surprise my mom at Christmas. No one asked me about Vietnam including my family, friends, and former coworkers. When I got home in March of 1972, it was the same thing. Nobody ask me about Nam the whole time I was home. Coming home after my tour adjustment was smooth because I still had more than 2 years to go with my enlistment. Once I got out of the service I never talked about Nam and no one asked me. I just went on with my life.

I like the 'Welcome Home' we get now but it is not the same as when we first came home. The thing I am most proud of is the recognition the troops are getting now. As a life member of Vietnam Veterans of America our motto is, *NEVER WILL ONE GENERATION OF VETERANS ABANDON ANOTHER VETERAN*. I feel we had a part in that happening. When I joined VVA in 1990 I was able to talk to other Vietnam Vets about Nam and they could relate. My wife and I go every year to the Vietnam Veteran's memorial in Baltimore, Maryland, and this year seemed a little harder to take.

Today I am married to a beautiful woman named Dottie. The end of June we will celebrate our 35th wedding anniversary. I have a beautiful daughter and 3 wonderful grown grandchildren. I've worked for a great company RKK Engineers in Baltimore for 22 years and am a member of VVA Chapter 451 and Treasure of the Maryland State Council of Vietnam Veterans of America. The lord has blessed me and I am so proud of my service.

The one thing I want to say is that I took this country for granted before I went through Jungle Survival School. One of the things we had to go through one night after completing the obstacle course was getting captured, interrogated, stuffed in small boxes, and eat sardines and rice. The next morning we were called out to bow to the commandant. As they were raising the American flag, someone shouted "Attention, about face," and the tears started rolling down my face.

It was in that moment I knew what that flag meant.

~ Dave Schofield, USAF, Vietnam Veteran

> "   We deserve a Purple Heart medal for Agent Orange
>
>   ~ Captain USAF Retired "
>
>   Vietnam Veteran

JOHN BACHOR

U.S. ARMY

"AS FAR AS READJUSTING I DON'T KNOW IF I EVER DID."

My name is John Bachor, and I am a Vietnam Veteran.

My Father served during WW2 as a flight Engineer and mechanic on a C-47 troop carrier, in the 435th Troop Carrier group. He released gliders over Normandy and a few other places. He did a lot. My mother and father moved to California from Little Neck, New York, when I six years old and divorced shortly thereafter. I didn't see or hear from my father until I was 23 years old. I had already come back from Vietnam and did not want to hear anything about war. I had a very bad taste in my mouth about everything. Everything!

I was looking forward to a career in automotive racing when I got drafted. I served with the 20th Engineer Brigade, 36th Engineer Battalion during 1967 and 1968. My MOS was Wheel Vehicle Mechanic. I was the second enlisted person stationed in the 36th and was placed in Headquarters Company. I was a PFC. Sometime later, a motor pool Sergeant was assigned to our company and then another PFC added to finish off the motor pool personnel. Neither of them was as proficient as I was as a mechanic. Before the Army I was involved in drag racing, engine building and general chassis tuning. I had much more knowledge in automobiles than they did. I also set up all of the procurement parts, paper work. The Sergeant didn't have much to do, so he wasn't around much. 'Headquarters Co.' and 'B' Co. shared the same building. 'B' Co. was a heavy equipment service company. I spent most of my time there because we had many very large wheeled, heavy equipment vehicles. While in Vietnam, I spent most of my time at the 'B' Co. shop as well. On our way to Vietnam, our ship stopped in Okinawa for refueling. The Sergeant missed the ship upon leaving. I never saw him again.

I'm not sure when I first came into contact with Agent Orange. It might have been when a Huey flew overhead spraying what was called mosquito repellant. Either there were many lies, or they just didn't know about Agent Orange. One day, a Captain asked if I could put together a portable high-pressure washer to remove 'that sticky stuff' off of the equipment, and I said "Sure". About a week later, we tried it out. It was near what we thought was an old rice patty that had water in it. It worked great with water all over the place. We got good and wet. Others came to wash "that sticky stuff" off of their vehicles and equipment.

Then, one day, some one with some brains, noticed what was being done. They stopped the operation and informed the guys, that it was our 'base camp water' supply. So we ate it, showered in it, brushed our teeth with it, had cooks mix our dried milk with it, potatoes, and so on. Now we know what it was, 'DOWS, AGENT ORANGE'.

The worst part for me was when I got off of the plane in Oakland, California. My reception back home was filled with rocks, bottles, piss bags, hollers, and Berkley students calling us baby killers. My mother asked me why I even came home. As far as my re-adjusting upon returning home, I don't know if I ever did.

I have a number of health issues, including having had three heart attacks. I have always been healthy and worked hard. The first heart attack was in 2002. I continued working at my regular job and kept up with my hiking and photography until the second heart attack in 2010, which caused me to become disabled. Then on Christmas Day 2011, I had the third heart attack, which took 47% of my heart, (LVF). After 2002 my METS level was 2.78. I should have received a 100% disability rating at that time, but the VA only gave me 10%. I have been fighting with the VA for 2 1/2 years now.

After the 2002 heart attack, I started looking for others with the same problems that I had. I found many, way too many. I started going to Veteran support groups. I also have "PTSD". I noticed there were a few members in our group that had Purple Heart medals. Don't get me wrong because I honor and respect those that have been awarded that very special medal. Since I can't go hiking and do my photography, like I once could, I'm too sick and weak to go climbing around the outback. The Purple Heart medal recipients, for the most part can still do it. They will probably live longer then I will. I wondered why we (those afflicted with Agent Orange), couldn't have a medal to show our wounds. To some degree, we died forty some years ago. It just hasn't caught up with most of us yet.

My cousin Joyce encouraged me a few years ago to design an image of an Orange Heart medal, so we could have it placed on t-shirts and other products to get the word out. We decided on Cafe Press to do the work. By doing this we would receive about 10% of the sales in profits, and then we could share with the Vet's and their families in need to help make their lives a little better.

Mostly because of Joyce's bubbly personality, and all of her friends and past experiences, this is getting bigger then we thought it would. To create more awareness for our cause, and give honor to our Agent Orange afflicted Veterans, we have a design and plan to have a beautiful Agent Orange Monument erected in Eisenhower Park, East Meadow on Long Island in New York. The group photo is my team, and we welcome your visits and donations @ agentorangeawareness.org.

I have made many friends because of this cause.

~ John Bachor, U.S. Army, Vietnam Veteran

> **"** Thank you for your service. For many, coming home was harder then being in the Nam **"**
>
> ~ Patriot

JAMES P. O'CONNOR

U.S. AIR FORCE

"A SOLDIER 'IN COUNTRY' DURING WAR WILL NEVER FORGET."

I was in Vietnam from 1968 to 1969.

I am standing in a guard tower here, M-16 in hand, keeping a look out for V.C. The Air Force Security police were the first Air Force Combat veterans with boots on the ground in any war. There is a detailed display of this at Wright Patterson AFB, in Fairborn Ohio. It's worth a visit. I was in the 35th Combat

Support Group at Phan Rang AFB, from February 1968 to 1969. We were hit with rockets the first night. Sometimes I remember TET, and sometimes it's cloudy. I do remember the dead, ground infiltration, and Spooky firing the Quad 30 caliber guns near the front gate. It looked like the fourth of July. Every 5th round was a tracer. Charlie was about to bust through the main gate. My greatest fear was a recurring dream I had while in Nam. The dream was a VC coming down on me with a knife, while I was asleep with the enemy overrunning the base.

I was in a firefight in the Delta area that lasted for seven hours. After the 'all clear', I walked by a dead body lying on the barbed wire fence with the abdomen blown out. I didn't realize the changes at first. I became angry quickly. For more then two years after returning home, if I was sleeping and fire sirens went off, my feet were on the floor before I was awake. The sirens were our warning of incoming rockets and mortars. The adjustments at home were something I never thought of very much. I did feel very much alone and abandoned by my peers. I began drinking heavily and having dreams of Vietnam. The alcohol enhanced the dreams of ground infiltration, and a helicopter crash, where 7 people burned to death, and walked through swampy areas of the base, slapping flares looking for Charlie. Finally I reached out for help from the VA. In 2005 I was diagnosed with PTSD. I remain in therapy to this day.

For decades I felt alone even with my first wife and two kids. I was happy for a while until my second wife abandoned me in 1998. I still don't know why, but she told me many years later that her leaving was not my fault. After living alone for the past 14 years, I have learned to survive once more.

If I hadn't sought help from the VA here in Dover, Delaware, I probably would never have contacted anyone about Nam. I can talk about some things now, but there are also some things that are still blacked out. At times when a buddy of mine, Johnny Sullivan, brings up certain things, it brings back more painful memories. I still shed tears when visiting the Vietnam wall in D.C. I felt anxiety at the memorial in Dover. A soldier who has been 'in country' during a war will never forget some of the experiences. After a soldier is home, they are still 'in country'. The war never goes away. The VA has helped me manage PTSD, through therapy since 2005. In 2010, I was diagnosed with prostate cancer from exposure to Agent Orange. The prostate had to be removed, followed by radiation therapy, and now I have residual issues with my bladder. There's no end to it. Nam stays with us one way or another. I can I honestly share internal scratches and stories with many.

This is a picture with John Wilkins and myself. The next photo shows the back of Beetle Bailey's shirt, which reads, "FIGMO". That stands for, "Finally I Got My Orders." He was on his way back to the 'world'. The picture was taken at our homemade watering hole at White Rock, National Park in Phan Rang. I was fortunate enough to be in touch with other Veterans whose memories brought a little light back into my life. I couldn't talk about Vietnam for 36 years. After I retired in 2003, I had a lot more time on my hands. I started having dreams about things I thought I'd forgotten. I turned to alcohol to forget, but dreams, the sound of the chopper's aircraft noise and fire sirens became worse and more frequent. In 2005, I finally got help from the V.A. in Dover, DE. I am still in counseling for PTSD and stopped drinking 6 years ago. Memories remain, but are easier to live with.

My first attempt to walk the 'Wall' was in 1992. I couldn't do it. I broke down and went back to my car in tears. On March 17 of 2006, I went back to the wall, only this time with a group of

Vietnam Vets who were in PTSD therapy with me. It was one hell of a bitter cold day. Looking out of my front window at 5 a.m., the ground and my car were covered with thick ice. I had a remote starter but I had to wait until the car warmed up. It took about 45 minutes before I could open the car door.

I drove 9 miles to Dover where we caught a bus for Washington, DC. We were all able to walk the 'Wall'. There were thousands of Vietnam Vets lined up along the entire memorial 'Wall' and every one of them held out their hand to shake ours and say, "Welcome Home". I never heard anyone say that when we came home from that forsaken place called Vietnam. I plan on walking the 'Wall' again. I'm not sure I can do it by myself. Just the thought of it gives me anxiety. Hell, visiting the Vietnam Memorial in Dover, DE with fellow chapter VVA 850 Vets brings a heavy heart to me.

I have never expected anyone or anything to change a situation for me. After seeing how many Veterans have prayed to save themselves, and seen fellow Veterans die or be physically and mentally damaged for life, it has let me know that I have to be the one to change the situation within myself. I am the only person responsible for curing myself. I reached out for guidance through behavioral health, and together I gathered the strength to face what I so desperately tried to drown out through self-medication with alcohol. There will be times when triggers from certain things will bring back the past. Learning the triggers is something we need help with from professionals.

Dealing with them is up to us.

~ Sgt. James P. O'Connor USAF Security Police, Vietnam Veteran

"
   I found out what happened when the GIs came home from Vietnam.

People would give gave them bad names, treated them like criminals and looked down on them. I don't understand that. I never heard anything about 'Baby Killer' and I've tried too many times to say otherwise. It was you who saved our babies, children, women and men from getting killed.

I know this because I am Vietnamese and I am here because of you!
"

~ Vietnamese civilian

LARRY SCHNITZLER-SPRIGGS

U.S. ARMY

"IT WAS A ROUGH TIME."

My name is Larry Schnitzler-Spriggs, and I'm a Vietnam Veteran.

I was drafted in March 1968 and was in NAM from August 68 to August 69. I was with the 8th Infantry Charlie CO 4th Infantry. Most of my time was up in the Central Highlands, Plekiu and Dak Toe area. I had over 100 combat flights on choppers and was wounded by shrapnel in an ambush. We were pinned down for 2 weeks somewhere near the Ho Che Min trail.

When we finally got out, the chopper that I was on took 9 rounds of AK. We had to land at the bottom of the hill and walk back through the jungle to find our company. It was a rough time. I am a proud Nam Vet and to me all Nam Vets are Heroes.

In May of 69, we were involved in a firefight with the VC. We were going through a village just checking to make sure there were no bad guys in the village. Things looked okay, but as we were leaving we began to get sniper rounds all around us. Then all hell broke loose. We hit the ground and started returning fire. It lasted about 20 minutes or so. We lost 3 men and killed over 25 VC. We went back to the village and rechecked it and found lots of AK-47 and B-40 Rockets and a storage of rice. It was all buried underneath a manure pile.

I am very proud to be a NAM Vet. I know the stuff that I went through and the things I've seen. It is by the hand of the Lord that I am here, not because of being RAMBO. My greatest fear was walking point. The one memory that has always stayed with me happened a week before going home. I was in base camp with a friend who got a truck. He wanted me to come along with him and say good-bye to our friends who were set up on a firebase about 20 clicks away. I already had said my good-byes and just wanted to go home, so he went by himself. The truck was hit by a B-40 rocket and blown up. My friend was killed instantly. I often wonder what stopped me from going with him. I would have been killed too. It seems to me that it must have been the man upstairs watching over me.

There is nothing but killing and suffering in the Nam story. Any Vet will tell you that. I was treated like crap when I came home. My own stepfather told me to quit feeling sorry for myself and when I went to move in with my favorite uncle, his wife threw me out. I was just a kid who wanted someone to say, "Welcome Home" and "Can we help you get started?". However, none of that happened for us NAM Vets. We still fight and shed a few tears. I've been fighting for 48 years, and I am tired. We are still fighting here at home, and I guess we will until we all die.

I have been retired for the last 4 years. I spend my time working around the house. Hunting deer and wild turkey in the fall with my bow and arrow, is my pastime. In the summer I play and coach a softball team and try to work out several times a week. I like to stay in the best shape I can.

~ Larry Schnitzler-Spriggs, U.S. Army, Vietnam Veteran

"   I was in the South Vietnamese Air Force and a crew chief on an American C-130 Hercules cargo aircraft.

I was very angry about what we had to endure after the collapse of South Vietnam, and couldn't believe on the last day, that America was really abandoning us. No one believed that this was really happening, but it was. On April 30th, 1975, the very same day that the United States pulled out, I was taken prisoner by the North Vietnamese and spent the next one and a half years in a prison camp in Vietnam. I escaped, stayed hidden, and somehow managed to build a boat to leave Vietnam with my wife and young son.

The boat sank, but the Malaysian Navy rescued us. "

~ South Vietnamese Soldier

JIM MARKSON

U.S. AIR FORCE

"I HAD NO IDEA WHAT I WAS IN FOR."

I was 19 years old when I arrived in Vietnam.

I was born in Hackensack, New Jersey. My mother was a Czechoslovakian Catholic with 11 brothers and sisters. Two of her brothers served in the Army during World War II. Her brother, 2nd Lieutenant Joseph Tengi, was killed just outside of Berlin. My middle name is Joseph named after him. Dad was born in Canada and migrated to the United States in the early 1900's. In 1916 he ran away from home, joined the Army, served in the infantry, and was wounded twice, and discharged under general conditions for misrepresentation of age. He was only 15!

My Father was Commander of The American Legion, Bill Brown Post in Brooklyn, NY. From 2011 to 2013, I became Commander of The Veterans of Foreign Wars Post 107, one of the oldest VFW posts in the United States, formed by World War One Veterans in 1919, which is also in Brooklyn.

I joined the United States Air Force in 1966 to become an Air Traffic Controller, but due to strict vision regulations was put into the Security Police career field. I later volunteered for Vietnam. I was full of bravado and adventure. After the TET Offensive in 1968, I couldn't get out of there fast enough. I had no idea what I was in for. As a Security Policeman we controlled all movement throughout the airport. Gates and checkpoints were everywhere. We stopped all vehicles except the "meat wagon", a sinister, dull, flat, black, painted truck, with wooden sides. It was covered with a loose fitting canvas that was kind of a spooky flap as it went by. It was like something from Ichabod Crane's Headless Horseman. It had no markings and kept the flashers on, day and night. Out of respect, no one stopped this vehicle. It got the priority it deserved. It carried the dead from the flight line to the mortuary, also located on Saigon Airport. Day and night C-7 Caribou's, C-123 Provider's, and C-130 Hercules cargo planes would come and go from Saigon. We knew that as the ramp opened there was always a possibility the cargo would be body bags from the field. I could not take my eyes off of them having boots sticking out of the bags in positions a living persons feet would not be in. Often the bodies were decayed and were starting to smell. The meat wagon always smelled which was another reason not to stop it at your gate. Knowing what the smell was would make me dry heave at times.

On the eve of the TET Offensive and during the onslaught that followed, the only substance in our veins was adrenaline, heavily laced with a sense of duty and honor. A sniper had found his way on top of the roof of a two- story aircraft maintenance hangar not far from my bunker. It was during a lull, eerie quiet, when all of a sudden he let loose on full automatic, and started spraying bullets at the aircraft that were parked on the flight line. He was to my nine o'clock position and less than 100 yards away, I considered it an easy shot. Without any thought, I left the bunker and set my M-16 sights for the roof, with finger on the trigger, waiting for the illuminating flares to do their job.

Coming home seemed like something I had been waiting for all my life. The thought of being a different person, never entered my mind, but I was. The reception from my family and close friends was really great. The general community's reception was far different and an unfortunate story. As Vietnam Veterans we hid, grew our hair long, wore bell-bottoms and love beads, and I even grew a beard. We kept our mouths shut and tried our best to fit in with whatever part of society we could. I can recall times when I was asked if I had been in Vietnam and I would just say "NO", and it would eat me up inside that I had chosen to answer as I did. For 25 to 30 years we hid, instead of coming out of the closet. We came out of the bunker when attitudes finally changed. As a group we weathered those years with dignity, comparable to none. We owe it to those who never came home and to the thousands that did come home and are no longer with us to tell the story.

PTSD is an insidious situation. The topic came up from time to time. But it wasn't until after 2007, when the 2nd childhood friend of mine, (both Vietnam Veterans from Sheepshead Bay), took his life, that I sought out psychiatric help from the Brooklyn, VA. Night terrors, alcohol consumption, intrusive memories, disturbed sleeping, exaggerated startle reaction, hyper-vigilance, isolation to avoid conflict, and inability to control tears from traumatic reminders, are just some of the 'insidious' things that took years to manifest.

Veteran services have improved dramatically since I was discharged in 1970. However, there is still tremendous work that still needs to be done. The delays for medical care and benefits are totally unacceptable.

I am semi-retired and self-employed and consider myself very fortunate. Many, many Vietnam Veterans who returned home have not done as well and are no longer with us. I consider myself a Veteran's Advocate. I take advantage every very chance I get to improve the status and welfare of Veterans.

As I write this I have never been prouder, than I am right now, to have been part of the Vietnam experience.

~ Jim Markson, USAF Vietnam Veteran and author of *VIETNAM And Beyond, Veteran Reflections*

"
    My husband came home from Vietnam a changed man in many ways.

We had only been married a little more than 2 years before he went over.

His year over there continues to cause problems in our lives today, over 40 years later, because of my husbands handling of Agent Orange. He also suffers with PTSD!

The impact of war affects the wife and family.
"

~ Vietnam Vet's Wife

Ronald D. Hurst

U.S. Army

"Many never really understood what Vietnam veterans went through."

I was deployed in August 1969 and was an Army demotion specialist with Charlie Company, 196th LIB, American Division, and stationed in Chu Lai, South Vietnam.

Like the rest of the other soldiers, I was very young and right out of high school. Seeing your fellow soldiers wounded or killed, and knowing that your time is coming, is a terrible part of war. There is a constant fear of never getting out alive, knowing that there is nothing you can do about it, or help the family that is left behind. War changed the way I thought about life. I no longer cared what happened or what people thought. The way I saw it, I had already been to hell and back. I was no longer the same 20-year old kid that left home in 1969. War took away my youth.

RONALD D. HURST

Pfc. Ronald D. Hurst is an army demolition specialist stationed in Chu Lai, South Vietnam. He has now completed three months of his 18-month tour.

He is the son of Mr. and Mrs. Henry Hurst, 3105 Hurst Road Auburndale.

My good friend, Danny Roberts got killed in Vietnam. I have stayed in touch with his mother and sister. When Danny was in Nam, he wrote a letter home naming his pallbearers because he had a feeling he wasn't coming home. Pictured in the group photo left to right is Daniel (Mac) McKinney, Capt. Bob Morris, Tom Felgenaker and myself. I don't recall the name of the fellow in front. I have great respect for Capt. Morris. He never asked his men to do anything that he wouldn't do himself.

There was no welcome home for our Vietnam Vets. If employers knew you were a Vietnam Vet, you could not get hired. But the government promised the draft dodgers work.

I tried to drown all of the past memories with alcohol, and of course that only worked until I sobered up. Then I would drink some more. God erased a lot of the memories, which I'm very thankful for. Like all other Veterans, when a chopper goes overhead, I instinctively stop and look up.

We would get mail and I would open Bill Young's letters from his wife and read just a little bit. Then I'd reseal them. When Bill would open his mail, I would ask about something in the letters. Bill never could figure out how I knew about certain things. I didn't tell him until many years later when we finally found each other after the war. I can't explain it, but I could sense that Bill needed my help and so I reached out to someone else in Ohio in search of him. I was right. Now I talk to Bill quite often. We are very close. This is a picture of Bill Young and I in March 2015. We attended the Vietnam reunion for the 196th.

When I got home I fought another battle. This time it was with the VA for 20 years just trying to get the help that I needed. For 18 years, the VA said they lost all of my records and kept saying there was nothing wrong with me and that it was all 'in my head.' I finally got help, but at a great cost. There are still a few bad days, but nothing like it was.

Life is a lot better now.

~ Ronald D. Hurst, U.S. Army, Vietnam Veteran

> " There are no survivors of war. "
>
> ~Patriot

Dennis Sprague

U.S. Army

"MY GREATEST FEAR WAS A WELL SET-UP AMBUSH."

I was born in St. Louis, Missouri in July of 1949.

My dad was an electrician and mom was a typesetter. I was a sheet metal worker at a local factory before getting drafted on May 16, 1969. I was sent to Ft. Leonard Wood, Mo. for Basic Training, and took AIT at Tigerland, Ft. Polk, Louisiana. I spent my tour of duty in Vietnam with Company D, 1/502 Infantry,

101st Airborne Division, and was stationed in I Corp. I finished my two-year hitch at Ft. Hood, Texas.

My dad served in the U.S. Navy from December 8, 1941 until the end of WWII. One of my sons served with the U.S. Navy from 2004 to 2008 as well. Dad didn't talk about the war very much. He was a crewmember of the USS Birmingham, a ship that was engaged in every major sea battle of WWII. Years after he had died, I was watching a TV show about Kamikaze attacks. One Kamikaze was filmed as he flew straight through all of the flack and slammed into the ship that the battle was being filmed from. That ship was dad's ship, the USS Birmingham, and he had never said anything about it. He was a true Hero. My Navy son served on the aircraft carrier Theodore Roosevelt in the War of Iraqi Freedom.

The physical regiment of Basic and AIT training was no big deal. We were all young and strong. The barracks consisted of cleaning, inspections, and card games. The Army chow was just fine. As for social life, there was drinking, some fighting, bar rooms, pool halls, bowling alleys, and some of the best friends a guy could have. All of this of course, was stateside. In the triple canopy of the jungle in Vietnam there wasn't any social life.

I was in the infantry in Viet Nam for one year. I did not see heavy action like a lot of guys did, but what I did see was enough. The U.S. Military can produce a tremendous amount of firepower, and the ensuing destruction is totality. Casualties are memories that you really don't want. We were like a family in the jungle. We would fight among ourselves, and we'd stick up for each other. The few times we got to the rear area, where we could sleep on cots, drink cold beer, and eat hot chow. If one of us got pushed, we would all push back. While in the military, I learned the value of leadership, teamwork, and respect for the chain of command. My greatest fear in Viet Nam was getting caught in a well set-up ambush. If I had been in one, chances are I wouldn't be here today. All I can say about war is that it never leaves you. I don't have many pictures of myself in Viet Nam, because most of them were lost over the years. In the picture of me sitting down, I'm the one eating the C-Rats. The GI sitting next to me was severely wounded and has been the subject of many prayers over the last 45 years. I would guess this is breakfast just before we packed up and moved out. It's just a spot in the jungle, but it looks like a well used spot, so I think it's close to an LZ (Landing Zone), for the choppers. My mother carried this picture with her everyday until I got back home.

I left Viet Nam in October of 1970. The reality of leaving was in strange conflict to my long-term expectation. We didn't leave at high noon, so we didn't see the brightness of a clear and decisive victory. We left in the darkness of an unfinished war that would just continue to be fought. And we left guys behind that were still fighting it. They were guys that to a man, wanted to come back home with honor. I had completed my tour and I wanted to go home. There's no doubt about that, but it left for lack of a better word, a lonely feeling in me. I can't really get a handle on it, but it's a feeling that has stayed with me, and probably always will. I think this feeling is shared with a lot of guys that were there. In the autumn of 1983, I put this feeling on paper the best I could when I wrote, 'Headin' Home'.

Headin' Home

There was an awareness both day and night
that you weren't a veteran 'till you made the flight,
and it was a long time coming.

Then it finally arrived, the day we were all hoping for,
the day to step off the distant shore of South Vietnam.
And step onto that "Giant Bird" and scream away
headin' home again.

My vision, or dream, and I think this was shared with others that
were there,
was to scream away at high noon so I could turn and stare,
at Vietnam behind me.

But it wasn't a day flight.
In darkness we left.
Just got aboard and flew away,
feeling like thieves in the night.

I say thieves and I say it willing.
The take-off was almost chilling.
It was quiet and austere, and no one dare make a sound.

It was a silent moment of care for our friends we left on the ground.
You'd think we'd be cheering to be young and alive and free and
headin' home,
instead we were praying that our friends would survive to get a flight
of their own.

But we'd never know and it's like we stole something they might need,
fighting support or fellowship, in the event that they might bleed.
I think this was shared, in unison we stared from the flying bus,
and as hard as we stared we could not see, Viet Nam behind us.

But we were alive and lucky and on a flight, and proceeded on into
the night.......headin' home...

For a brief time I worked traffic check point between Pohl Bridge
and Fire Base Birmingham. A Vietnamese woman set up a little
roadside food stand not far from our checkpoint. She had a little
boy with her and the little boy would come over and get real
close to us. She was very young and I asked if he was her little
brother. She told me that he was just a little kid from her village.
She said his dad was an ARVN soldier, and he and his mother
and grandparents were killed in a VC raid on his village. The
little boy was only three years old and had no family. He ate
when people would offer food and he slept wherever he could.
He was on his own. Maybe it was a line, maybe not, but I bought
some food she was selling and he sat on my lap and ate it. He was
a beautiful little boy and I think of him often. He would be close
to fifty now and I pray that he is. He was just a little kid caught
up in a war, but I will never forget him.

The picture of me standing was taken at a Catholic Monastery
that we were guarding. It was kind of a casual picture that was
deliberately taken for mom and dad. Notice the clean-shaven face
and combed hair. The church only got hit at night. I was in the
infantry in the north part of Vietnam for one year.

My family reception was nice back home, but not so much by the community. The "Welcome Home" and "Thank you" didn't happen when it meant something. Now, 40 to 50 years later, we're a bunch of old guys and society is nicer to us.

I grew up with Heroes, my dad, his friends, my uncles and their friends. They were all the same. They came back from saving the world, and without saying much, picked up their shovels and hammers and built this Great Nation that we all know as America.

I look forward to retiring in the next few months and writing a book about my grandfather who led an incredible life.

~ Dennis Sprague, U.S. Army, Vietnam Veteran

" Their names are carved in stone, never to touch our tears again.

Lest we forget, lest we grow old, our hearts must never be so cold.

And we must not run and hide, we must remember them,

The boys who died...

~ Danielle Steele, author of "

Message From Nam

KENNETH BOPP

U.S. ARMY

"FACING THE WALL AND A STORY OF HEALING."

My name is Kenneth Bopp, and I am a Vietnam Veteran.

I could tell a war story as well as the next guy. I thought I was home free and did not have any problems. Most of the pictures of that time are either missing or put away in some box and are never brought out; Just like the traumatic memories have been placed aside as well, I remained at ease with my life that way. I served with the U.S. Army, 44th Medical Brigade, 24 Evacuation Hospital, and USARV.

Then something happened that shook me to my foundation. It did not come from another Veteran, my family, any friends or co-workers. It came in the mail, in a plain brown wrapper in the form of the National Geographic VOL. 167, NO. 5 May 1985. I will remember that day as long as I live, for that was when I realized who I was and where I had been. 'The Wall' had been in existence for almost two and a half years, and I really knew nothing of it. As I read alone, I found myself having to really struggle to see the print. I suddenly realized that I was trying to read through tears, which eventually turned into racking sobs that frightened me. I struggled with these new feelings of unrest. I felt the family was walking on eggshells, as if they were afraid that anything they said or did would send me off on another crying jag. I found I could not listen to any music from the sixties, or of that era on the radio. I always found myself crying. I tried not listening to the radio, but the music was in my head all the time.

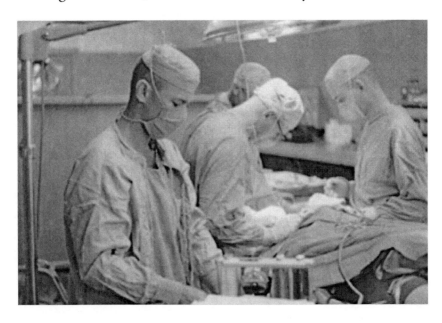

With help, I came to the conclusion that the only way to heal, was to visit 'The Wall', and that visit must be made alone. I arrived in D.C. on a Sunday and headed for the 'Vietnam Veteran's Memorial.' Shaking off the strange feeling that enveloped me, I walked up the slight rise and looked around for the listing book to look up the names I wanted to visit. All of a sudden, I found myself shaking. I turned around and walked back to the bike. After smoking a couple of cigarettes, I again walked toward the listing book. Again I started shaking and decided to approach the memorial from the other side. I stood looking at the statue of the three troopers and still felt fairly calm. The stark beauty of 'The Wall' struck me. It was magnificent. I could actually see the reflection of the visitors, even through the tears in my eyes. I approached the listing book and looked up the names of those I wanted to visit, and finally began my walk along 'The Wall.' The first name I went to was that of a family member of a friend. Stepping back, I spoke to him, explaining how I happened to be there and my gaze took in the many names carved around his. I began to cry, silently with a blinding realization that I might have taken care of some of these men during my tour in Vietnam. I did not remember even one of the names, or faces of those placed in my charge as a nurse anesthetist! I finally remembered one trooper that I was caring for in the emergency ward at 3rd Surg. He had multiple fragmented wounds of the abdomen and a wound on one eye. The eye wound was deemed not serious enough to transfer him to another unit for eye surgery yet, because he needed his belly taken care of first. He kept saying, "What a terrible way to die". I told him his wounds were not that severe, and that he was not going to die. He eventually calmed down and stopped talking about dying. As the bearers came to take him, he looked at me, grabbed my hand, and blood began pouring from the eye wound, his mouth, nose and ears. He died. I had unknowingly, lied to him by telling him he was going to be all right. Feeling desolate, the tears flowed freely as I apologized to them all.

I returned to "The Wall' the next morning, and after a few minutes of meditation approached one of the volunteers who recognized me from the day before. They saw the behavior of a first timer and always kept an eye on them. Maybe I was not alone in this thing after all. Directing me to a spot that would serve my purpose, someone said, "Welcome home, brother". Except for my family on my return, not one person had welcomed me home. Perhaps I was "coming home" finally. I placed my letter in the fissure between two of the panels and stepped back. Of course there were more tears, but they were more of a balm than the acid I had been enduring since reading the National Geographic issue.

I then saw a great bear of a man in a wheelchair. He had no legs. He had on a baseball cap and vest, both covered with pins, medals, and patches. Our eyes met, and I offered my hand, saying, "Welcome home, brother". We exchanged unit designations and locations 'in country'. He asked me how I felt after my visit to "The Wall". I told him of my feelings of guilt and sorrow for not remembering names and faces of those I cared for. He said, "You did something over there, and I am sure you did it to the best of your ability. Had you not been there, who knows how many of us would not have come home at all. All of you that were there to help the wounded did a difficult job. You feel guilty because you came home, and they did not, because you did not do as tough a job as others, but that is just not true. None of us that were there liked anything about what we were doing, but we did it. And I feel we are the better for it".

I thanked him, and asked how he became so perceptive. He said he spent a lot of time around 'The Wall,' had talked to a great many people and heard many stories, and said the way I felt was one of the more prominent feelings among the medical personnel located in hospitals. It was evident in the way they spoke and looked. Thanking him again, I left as I had a long trip home to New Orleans.

On my bike return home, I was so high after my visit, I found myself screaming to the sky, "I'm alive. I'm alive. Thank God, I'm alive." We soldiers went to Nam together and some of us came home together, but none of us came back whole. Thanks to those that conceived 'The Wall', in the face of daunting odds, we veterans now have a healing place to visit.

This picture is of an awards ceremony where I believe we all received the ACM, Army Commendation Medal. I also received a Purple Heart medal for wounds received on a previous deployment. Pictured left to right: Col. Robert Leaver, unknown, myself, Peggy Perri and Linda Troeger.

I have recently been diagnosed with End Stage Renal disease as a result of diabetic nephropathy. I have been told that I will have to go on dialysis within 6 months. Diabetic nephropathy is atypical, in that there is no accompanying retinopathy or neuropathy. I was stationed in Long Binh, which was one of the most heavily sprayed areas with Agent Orange.

~ Kenneth Bopp, U.S. Army, Vietnam Veteran
Healing Tribute: http://youtu.be/s-N0B0WMid0

" The fear of danger existed every night of our year of duty.

I am proud of my service in an unpopular war. The military had several thousand, specially trained dogs that were in Vietnam and were euthanized upon America's withdrawal.

Most of us didn't learn about their fate for twenty years. It was a sad day. They deserved better.

We have been dedicating monuments to their memory around the country ever since then. **"**

~ Steve Janke, Vietnam Vet

BILLY GRAMLIN

U.S. AIR FORCE

"MY BEST FRIEND OVER THERE WAS MY DOG."

Vietnam presented a wide array of combat challenges, for the large variety of soldiers, sailors, Airmen, and Marines who served there.

I would like to say that I am proud to have served and I am thankful I lived through my time in the war, and made it home in one piece. Having been in the Air Force, I don't want to sound as though I am claiming honor and valor that I did not earn, but on the other hand, there are men from other service branches who have the tendency to think and say, that all of the Air Force and Navy guys had it easy. I don't dispute that claim when compared to the hot firefights and jungle combat that many of those guys were exposed to, but you could get wounded or killed in a lot of different ways just by being 'in country.'

Incoming rockets didn't care what your job description was. Since the VC and North Vietnamese were shooting at aircraft on the flight-line and barracks where the crews and maintenance people slept, you could be killed in your sleep, or in the middle of a large air base like Da Nang with defensive security completely surrounding you. I saw that happen one night in 1971 when one building took a direct hit from two 122mm rockets. The aircraft maintenance crews were already asleep and didn't have enough warning to get out and into a bunker in time. Thankfully, most were saved, but we did lose some guys in that attack.

I was a United States Air Force Sentry Dog handler with the 366th Security Police Squadron, K-9 Division. We defended the base perimeter and the Air Force bomb dump at Da Nang Air Field in what was then, The Republic of South Vietnam. My dog King and I posted out between perimeter bunkers that were manned by United States Marines. I had to remind myself often that this was what they referred to as "the rear area", because when they were not in those bunkers they were "out there" in the bush, where the serious combat was. Make no mistake about it; I saw all the combat through random attacks from the enemy that I cared to see. Rockets and wild, pot shot small arms fire, coming across and through the perimeter fence, was not uncommon. Every rocket attack produced paranoia on the line that might be followed by a massive ground attack. Fortunately, I was never engaged in a firefight on the perimeter, which meant that every man and dog on that line would become expendable. We were between the enemy and any responding forces coming out to repel the attack. Ergo, my name is not etched in the wall.

One night when I got silhouetted against a fire burning in the base dump, that lay between my post and the base flight line, I came very close to taking a kill shot when an AK-47 round missed my head by mere inches. It might have been more like centimeters! It's a very uneasy and sickening feeling to hear what sounds like a supersonic bumblebee fly by your head, close enough to move your short hair, and have your ears hear the crack of the round leaving the muzzle. There's this sudden rush of realization that, 'THAT was freaking CLOSE!'

In some rocket attacks the rockets all passed over my post and fell deep in the base interior. I was thankful they weren't falling on me. It was scary hearing them go over, knowing how devastating they were, and seeing the damage they caused in the distance. Sometimes it seemed as if they were just thrown at us ad hoc, but they could be deadly accurate. I guess it depended on who was firing them. I watched a C-130 take a direct hit in the center of the fuselage, right between the two main wings one night while it sat on the tarmac. I don't think anybody was on board at the time. Sometimes it was as if they were shooting right at the post we were on, as if they were trying to blow out the fence. It was a scary feeling to have 122mm rockets hitting the ground all around you, looking like a grand finale fireworks display gone wrong, while they were all going off on the ground instead of up in the air and spitting hot steel and high explosives that literally bounced myself and my full-grown German shepherd off of the ground. We were vying for space in a shallow low spot on the ground, hoping it wouldn't be a shared grave. For an Air Force guy, I saw just enough combat to make me know that it must have been terrifying hell when the Marines went "out there" to face and kill the enemy! It is no surprise to me when I hear one of those guys talk about suffering from PTSD and other combat related stresses. I will never forget that most of the real heroes have their names etched on a wall in Washington DC.

My last and undoubtedly hardest day in Vietnam was saying goodbye, not just to my best friend, but a five-year combat Veteran. I rotated out in October 71, but I had to leave King. The

Air Force rotated their Military Working Dogs from handler to handler, but I will always remember King X765 who was fondly called 'Puppy King' for his puppy like face.

~ Billy Gramlin, USAF Vietnam Veteran

> "   Your sacrifice will not be forgotten.
>
> God's good graces got us through, and those that gave the ultimate shall live in my thoughts as long as I live. "
>
> ~ Patriot

PAUL MCNALLY

U.S. MARINE CORPS

"I WAS DESTINED TO BE A MARINE."

My name is Paul McNally, and I am a Marine Corps Vietnam Veteran.

I served from March 1965 to March1969 and did my tour in Nam from October 1966 to June 5, 1967. This photo is when I graduated from boot camp. In this group photo, which was taken just before we left the Chu Lai area, I'm the little guy, second from the left, holding my walking stick.

Our group was on the Chu Lai air base when the 196th started to move in, as we prepared to move further north into the Que Son Valley. Union operations were considered the fifth worst battles of the Vietnam War. They changed everyone, who fought with them. The Que Son Valley was where these operations took place and replays in my mind on a daily basis. It probably will for the rest of my life. The 5th Marines were the most decorated unit in the Marine Corps during the war. I wrote a book, called The Best of the Best, The Fighting 5th Marines Vietnam, over many years ago to try to understand my crazy life before, during, and after Nam and the Marine Corps. As one review proclaimed, I was destined to be a Marine.

I was awarded the Silver Star for one day and night of many battles that went on for over a month. Acts of valor were a common trait among the Marines who fought in them. We were just trying to keep each other alive and not be Hero's. I can give an idea of what that month was like for me. I started off the Union operations as a PFC rifleman, and before they were over, I was meritoriously promoted twice, the first time to L/Cpl. and given a fire team to run.

After the battle of May 12th and 13th, the second time I was promoted to Cpl. and given a squad to run. I was ready to run a fire team. I wasn't so sure about running a squad. The main reason I got these promotions was because our company Delta, 1/5 was nearly wiped out in the May battle that began on June 2, 1967 with the Union II battle. I did some crazy things in that battle. The witnesses of what I did that day and night, were both killed later on in the battle.

It was a mix of emotions changing from moment to moment. The fear was always there. During the May 12th battle, I felt very little fear. The same feelings were with me when I got shot on June 2, 1967. It was after I was shot and got back in line that I had time to think about what I had gone through. The reality of it all finally sunk into my thoughts. The fear gripped me and took hold pretty bad, lasting for several hours. As nearly fifty NVA soldiers were making their way to our position, I thought I was looking at what was going to kill me very shortly. We were not able to stop it from happening, and were nearly out of ammo and time, when the radio operator finally got in direct contact with a F-4 phantom jet with a Marine flying it. We were able to pinpoint our position with only pop-up flares and the jet was able to drop Napalm on the attacking NVA soldiers coming at us. This gave us our chance to get out of where we were, and meet up with what was left of our company. Soon after, we did get to some safety. The total firepower of the Marine Corps was unleashed on the enemy. When that type of firepower is coming down within a hundred yards of you, it will scare the hell out of you. This firepower was coming down for hours, and all I could do was lay flat on the ground and try digging a hole with my good arm.

Almost getting killed didn't stop in Vietnam. My book has all these additional situations in it.

Once a Marine, Always a Marine.

~ Paul McNally, USMC Vietnam Veteran and author of *The Best of the Best, The Fighting 5th Marines Vietnam*

> " The eye of an eagle, the heart of a lion, and the hand of a woman. The nurses took great care of us. "
>
> ~ Vietnam Veteran

ELLEN DIDERICH ZIMMER

U.S. ARMY

"I LOVED TAKING CARE OF CRITICALLY ILL PATIENTS."

"My name is Ellen Diderich Zimmer, and I am a Vietnam Veteran.

As I was working my way through college, I saw an advertisement about the Army's, Student Nurse Program. After checking into it, I decided to apply for it. I had been inspired to do something for my country when I heard JFK's inaugural address. I was very idealistic and patriotic, and wanted to help take care of the soldiers in Vietnam. I was accepted into the Student Nurse Program in 1968 and the Army paid for my last two years of college. I had to sign a 3-year service contract, in which I agreed to serve 3 years in the Army following graduation.

When I went into the Student Nursing Program, I was technically a PFC and graduated in March of 1970. A few days later, I was sworn in as a 2nd LT. This was at the height of student protests over the war. There were bombings and student riots on most college campuses. The Army recruiter was not allowed on the California State campus where I was a nursing student. I didn't tell any of my instructors or fellow students about my plans after graduation for fear of retaliation or humiliation. I remember when I was sworn in. It was almost in secret for fear of war protestors. My family thought I had made a horrible mistake.

After basic training at Ft Sam Houston, I was transferred to the Fitzsimmons General Hospital in Denver, CO. I was assigned to their ICU Recovery/Heart room. I loved taking care of critically ill patients, and it was there that I volunteered to go to Vietnam. I arrived 'in country' June of 1971, and was assigned to the 3rd Field Hospital. I was very upset with the assignment because I wanted to work on the front lines. I actually have nothing but bitter memories of my time there. The morale was very poor. There were a lot of problems with alcoholism and drug use by the GI's. I soon learned to hate the Vietnamese. I became a victim of violence, sexual harassment and sexual assault from the GI's that I was there to take care of. The war began to wind down and troops were being sent home, and thankfully I was sent home 3 months early in March of 1972.

The 9 months that I was in Vietnam affected the rest of my life. Before getting off the airplane in San Francisco when I returned, we were strongly advised to go to the nearest bathroom in the terminal and change out of our uniform into civilian clothes. War protestors were stationed at the front of the terminal and had been very hostile to returning soldiers. They liked to call us "baby killers". I rarely spoke to anyone about Vietnam including my family. They didn't ask any questions, as they had been advised not to ask us about Vietnam. I found out quickly that no one wanted to hear about it. It was at that time, one of the most controversial issues in our country.

My next duty station was at Ft Leonard Wood, MO. I was the head nurse of a six bed ICU. I was a very good nurse and was promoted to CPT. I completed my 3 year service obligation and was 'Honorably Discharged'. I thought I'd left Vietnam in my past. After marrying and starting a family, I began teaching nursing and absolutely loved it. A few times a year, I would get depressed and anxious. I attributed it to being over worked and stressed. While working full time teaching, I went back to school. I drove 126 miles one way to UCA one night a week for four years by myself to obtain a Master's Degree in nursing. I helped start the first 'Distance-Learning' Nursing Program, in Arkansas. I also published several nursing articles, wrote NCLEX questions, four different times for Nurse License Exams, and was a part time Nursing Consultant on several projects.

I thought everything was going well. I just didn't realize I had a deep-seated cancer, called 'Vietnam' that was about to cut me off at my knees. The earlier symptoms I had been able to write off as stress, morphed into full-blown PTSD. I had frequent flashbacks and nightmares almost every night. I became quite paranoid, anxious and severely depressed. My physical health deteriorated, and in August of 1999 I had to quit a very promising career. I could no longer function. PTSD completely took over my life. I thought I was the only person that this had happened to, but later found out this same scenario of delayed PTSD, was a common denominator in many of the nurses who had served a tour of duty in Vietnam. I have been receiving treatment for PTSD from the VA sine 1996. I continue to live my life such as it is, with support from my family and friends. I have good days and bad days and I take it one day at a time, by putting one foot in front of the other.

I left part of my soul in Vietnam. I've been trying to get it back home for the last fifty years.

~Ellen Zimmer, U.S. Army, Vietnam Veteran

"
    I care about the Vietnam Veterans as people, fathers, grandfathers, husbands, sons, brothers, and men.

Our country let you down. I never will.

You are all in my heart and in my prayers. My son volunteered to go to Iraq. I made sure he knew about Vietnam before he made this decision. He understands a lot more now than he did 8 years ago.

You are all my Heroes

"

~ Veteran's mother

VICTOR MICHAEL GARCIA

U.S. AIR FORCE

"I KNEW SOME OF THE GUYS THAT DID NOT MAKE IT HOME."

My name is Victor Michael Garcia.

At 16 years old, I knew full well that I was going to be drafted. The Vietnam War was all over the television. My oldest brother Reuben was a Master Sergeant in the 82nd Airborne as a Combat Medic. He is the recipient of a Purple Heart and Bronze Star with Oak Leaf Clusters, and has many more medals. I am very proud of him. He was home on leave and told me about the Vietnam War first hand. He knew what I should expect because he had completed two tours.

Many of the guys during that time decided to dodge the draft by running off to Canada or somewhere else. The parents of some high school guys were able to get college deferments. I was not, so I went to the recruiter's office and signed up. I graduated January 1968, mid-term from high school, and was in boot camp by July of that same year.

After boot camp, I arrived at my first base where I was trained as an Aircraft Fuels Specialist refueling and defueling aircraft. I tested fuels for water, rating fuel octane, and worked in the Fuel storage tank farm. Shortly after completing on-the-job and getting married, I received my orders for Vietnam in October of 1969.

I told my brother that I got my orders and where I was going. He let me know he was going to stop by and visit me to see me off. However, the Red Cross notified my base that my brother was killed in an automobile accident. He passed away one week before his birthday and four months before I shipped off to Vietnam. My Commanding Officer gave me emergency leave to attend his funeral. My father, myself and my other brother attended his funeral. Reuben received a hero's 21-gun salute. I cried.

I was 19 years old when I landed at Bien Hoa. After reporting to my CO, I got assigned to the Pacific Air Command, 3rd Combat Support Group, working in the fuel storage tank farm, refueling aircraft. I volunteered to work on the Barge Crew, unloading fuel barges on the Dong Nai River just outside Bien Hoa City. I also volunteered for augmented duties with base security. I felt that this was a chance for me to really help the war effort and support our base, as best I could in case of another TET Offensive.

When I landed at Bien Hoa air base, I was not yet quite a man, but old enough to do the unthinkable. I grew up quick and learned fast. Staying on constant alert, going with little sleep, waiting for incoming rockets, and protecting the fuel barge from attack on the river, was the hardest thing I ever did at 19 years of age.

When I was finally discharged in 1972, I had problems getting a job. No one liked Vietnam Vets. There were no jobs. All I had was my high school diploma, and what I learned in the Military.

I still have a hard time forgetting the war and things that occurred. I have PTSD with nightmares and trust issues. I also have guilt because I came home and so many of us did not. It hurts inside. I knew some of the guys that did not make it home. I watched bodies in black bags being loaded onto C-130's go home. I witnessed the blank stares of those guys coming back from the field. I saw one of our troops burned so badly, his skin was peeling off. I saw incoming mortars from VC explode less than 100 yards from me and I thought I would die. I have had multiple marriages. I drank heavily. It has taken me forty plus years to admit to myself that I needed help.

I only want to tell the story that is the truth, with the facts as they happened. I want to help pay things forward. I want to somehow let God know that I'm not a bad man and only did what was expected of me during this conflict. I want to help whomever I can, and however I can. I don't want to cry anymore in my sleep and have my wife wake me up. I don't want to see a war movie and start crying, and feel the need to walk away because I am ashamed. I finally went to the VA and got the help I needed, and I continue to work hard at it.

Before I served in the military, my name was Victor Michael. After being discharged from the military, I decided to add my father's last name of Garcia. I was teased about having two first names when I was in.

I pray that God forgives me for my actions. I pray that all of our Fallen Veterans are with God in peace. I also pray that those families who lost sisters, brothers, wives, husbands, mothers or fathers, have been able to find peace. Truth, trust and integrity mean everything to me.

For the past 20 years, Stand Down Sacramento sets up a camp to help homeless Veterans get off the streets. They help them with medical, dental, food, clothing, and assist in getting them housing, and locked in with the VA. Many of them are able to get disability benefits for themselves and their families. There are also many homeless female Veterans. It's shameful that veterans end up like this. I encourage you to visit http://standdownsacramento.org.

I wrote this poem after Preston Bleak, a Vietnam Veteran who was suffering from the early stages of Alzheimer's and homelessness, died at the age of 61.

MY COUNTRY TIS OF THEE

I Fought To Keep You Free
I Left My Home Confused and Bewildered
And I Returned Angry and Skeptical
I fought with Pride and I Stood My Ground

I Never Wavered In The Face Of Danger
I fought for you to be Free
How could you? Why would you not remember me?

Isolated, alone and in the night
On A Cold Alley Street
No warmth, No Light, No Food, No Wife
No Children to Hug Him Tight

All He Wants Is To live His Life
For You To Know How Hard he fights
With Dignity, With Might

My God Said
I will Comfort Thee
I will Love Thee
I will Show Thee The Light

But In The Alley
There is No Light
There Is No Love
There Was No One

To Show Him
There Is No Need To Fight Any Longer
But To Survive For Yourself
And Only You

If One and Only One
Would Have, Could Have Said
May I Help You?

~ Victor Michael Garcia, USAF, Vietnam Veteran

" You have just given other vets a reason to open up without feeling odd or less than a man.

We are all here to listen, to hug and to be forever in your debt. We are proud and aware, that war is terrible for soldiers and their families.

I know. My dad is a WWII Vet and my son is a Persian Gulf Vet with PTSD **"**

~ A Veteran's Daughter and Mother

JAMES THOMAS QUICK

U.S. ARMY

"WALTER CRONKITE INTERVIEWED ME IN THE JUNGLES OF VIETNAM."

My father was a South Carolina sharecropper.

I remember my feet were bound by rags and plowing behind a mule at age 17. After seeing the planes flying out of Ft. Bragg, I tried to enlist, but my parents needed me to work the farm. I was tired of that lifestyle and always looking at the tail end of a donkey. I aspired to be more and have more in life.

As soon as I turned 18 in 1949, I enlisted and entered the 82nd Airborne Division at Ft. Bragg. I was sent to fight in Korea and remember how frail looking the Korean troops were. Later, I was stationed in Japan, Germany and stateside too. I married and had 4 children, all who lived at Ft. Campbell, KY. My eldest daughter, Brenda, didn't even know what a civilian was until we moved to off-post housing in Clarksville, TN, March of 1964. That is when my first tour began in Vietnam as an Infantry Sky Soldier. Back then we did 18-month tours, and I was there from 1964 to 1966. I was 35 years old. I volunteered for the second tour and my wife pleaded with me and begged me not to go. But I responded by saying, "I know what I'm doing! There's nothing but kids going over there!" I was very protective of the men I served with. By this time many of the young men were the same age as my own children. I left and was gone from 1967 to 1969. I was in the Iron Triangle in Ben Cat. All in all, I served with the U.S. Army from September 1949 to April 1970.

Walter Cronkite interviewed me in the jungles of Vietnam. It was a filmed report on wounded American soldiers in Vietnam, shown on the Huntley-Brinkley NBC news, revealing that I had been wounded in action. I had been wounded in the leg and was expected to be out of action for some time, but wanted to return to my platoon and continue fighting. At the time, I was a platoon sergeant with the 173rd Airborne Brigade in Vietnam, and was concerned for the soldiers in my command.

Here is part of a letter that I wrote home:

"Have calmed down a bit since writing earlier. I was listening to the radio tonight and learned that all kinds of demonstrations and protests are going on against what we are here for. I know one thing, those sorry _ _ _ doing the protesting are communist or communist inspired. I don't want anyone to ever question or remark about U.S. forces being here. I just couldn't take it, with what we are going through."

I saved the following article, which speaks to the racial divide of Brothers fighting side by side in Vietnam and the divide in the United States.

My God ... How Can It Be?

My God . . .How Can It Be? . . .That one boy lies rotting from malnutrition and torture in a jungle prison camp in North Vietnam — and another boy spits and tramples on the flag of this country on the steps of a university of learning? . . . .

That one boy lies sightless in a U. S. Naval hospital from Communist - inflicted f a c e wounds — and another boy uses a Communist flag to drape himself in defiance of the laws of this country? . . .

That one man of medicine begins his thirtieth straight hour standing over an operating table in pursuit of life for men serving this country — and another man of medicine implores crowds of young men to refuse to serve their country? . . .

That one Negro holds the face of his dead white comrade in his arms and cries pitifully in a dirty mud hole in Vietnam — and another Negro screams with hate against his white brother in the streets of countless American cities? . . .

That one boy lies in a coffin beneath the ground because he believed in duty to his country — and another boy lies on a dingy cot giving blood to the enemies of his county? . ..

That one man of God shields a wounded boy from an enemy bayonet with his body and dies — and another man of god uses his cloth as a shield to preach hate, dissension and lawlessness? . ..

MY GOD, how can it be?

— NAVAL SERVICE Magazine

I know that my family and kids back home got to watch me on the news. But it sure would be nice to get the link to that Walter Cronkite interview, so my kids and grandchildren could see it. However, I don't know how to go about that. My daughter Brenda always watched the show 'The Rifleman', with Chuck Connors and said that I looked like him because of the high cheekbones. My wife's mother used to have prophetic dreams and saw me getting blown up. She called all the church members together to pray for my safety. There was in fact an explosion. A bomb fell out of the sky and landed next to me. I was a platoon leader at the time and speaking to 4 other men who perished. When I came to, everything was on fire. I had blood coming of my ears and nose. I thought I was in hell.

When my kids were little, they would ask me, "What is it like to kill someone?" I told them, "It was going to me or him and it wasn't going to be me". They would also ask, "Where were you in Vietnam?" I told them, "Hell, I was all over the damn place." I retired in April 1970 at the age of 39. The Army was changing and didn't seem to want soldiers like they did before. I was now faced with two skills; Farming and infantry. Neither one appealed to me anymore. I worked as a manager of Civilian KP services on post and didn't like it. Then I got into trucking to make a living, which I liked. Being on the road gave me lots of time to reflect about life and the choices I made. Post Traumatic Stress manifested early on, with explosive anger over many years, which finally resulted in my marriage ending, just shy of 30 years. The anger affected the family and myself. My daughter Brenda, told me many years later, her feelings from childhood. When they saw me come home they would go to their bedrooms because it was a refuge from the fighting. They were raised with PTSD and became hyper sensitive to my moods. When they were little and I was trying to do something, I would become enraged when they would gather around me. When the memories of war would surface, there would be resurgence in my drinking. It has been a vicious cycle.

I remarried and have out lived all of my siblings. I often wonder why I am still here. My daughter says that I'm still here to get to know my children and grandchildren, and for them to get to know me. The kids make fun of me. I have their pictures and clippings in my wallet in order of their age, somewhat like a file cabinet. They say I must have been a soldier in many lifetimes and tell me, "Job well done, Daddy." I guess once a soldier, always a soldier.

I had my 84th birthday this year and after all that I have seen and endured, I often wonder how I am still here. My health has seriously declined. I recently had surgery that went well, but I still have some trouble breathing. I have ailments caused from Agent Orange. When my time comes, I will be donating my body to science.

I hope that research will bring insight and understanding to what Agent Orange does to the body and give new recognition to those affected by it.

~ James Thomas Quick, U.S. Army, 82nd Airborne, Korea and Vietnam Veteran

> **“** My husband died in Nam and so for 46 years I tell every Vet I see, Welcome Home! **”**
>
> ~Vietnam Vet Widow

MICHAEL D. "MOON" MULLINS

U.S. ARMY

"OUR GOVERNMENT SENT US TO FIGHT AND THEN TIED OUR HANDS."

I volunteered to be drafted with the U.S. Army and departed on 10/7/67.

My training was at Fort Campbell. The MOS assigned to me was 11/C and 11/B with my primary objective as a mortar man and then grunt. I did advanced infantry training at Fort Polk,

Louisiana, in Tiger Ridge. I flew into Ben Hoa around the 25th of March 1969. This picture is with me on bunker guard duty. I think it was on one of our river outposts.

Camp Frenzel-Jones was my unit's main base camp. I was there maybe 4 times that year, including when I left. We built several forward operating bases and moved on. A few of the locations were located at an ARVN Fort; French Rubber Plantation in Tay Ninh Province, and a firebase named Stephanie. We also went to Phuc Vinh to support the 101st Airborne. Our unit went to Dak To and I think a village called Phu Duoc. We moved constantly and stayed in the boonies almost my entire time there. After the spring and TET in 1968, our brigade was tasked with patrolling all routes into Saigon, so we moved incessantly. My job was always the same. I was a grunt during the day. On night ops, was when we performed as a weapons platoon, supporting our patrols with mortar cover and illumination.

This is a picture of myself looking out over the rice patties. It was a very wet day. We did search and destroy missions in several areas.

Our problems were the same as any grunts in any war. There was constant stress, jungle critters, wading the rice paddies, sometimes supplies, sometimes water, always malaria, dysentery, laying concertina wire, walking, walking, and more walking. The monsoon season was a joyous time as we splashed around.

One of the funniest stories was the night we were in our bunkers and rain had been pouring down for hours. I felt something slither across my stomach and yelled, "SNAKE!" Three of us went nuts slashing with our machetes in the dark. We destroyed the sandbags in our structure but somehow missed each other. Looking out for each other was our most important job.

The Vietnamese people were poor. They mostly just wished both sides would go away so they could raise their crops. I don't remember working with the ARVNs that often. Once, the Koreans attached some of their White Horse Rangers to us. Those were bad dudes. My first operation and patrol was a major learning experience. We were hit by an ambush and the combat reporter traveling with us got hit in the thigh. It was a painful wound. He could not be evacuated because it was dusk. During the night he kept screaming and crying. Our medics had to dose him with morphine because he was pinpointing our location. It was a bit concerning and the more experienced men were rather disgusted by it. They did not mean to be harsh and wanted to survive the night. I also had my first experience with a leech during that same night. One got on my stomach right next to my navel. I yelled and an older grunt grabbed me and pulled me down. He asked me if I was trying to get myself killed. Next, he taught me how to deal with it. Pour dry salt on it if you have any at all, or hold a lit cigarette butt on it. It will drop off quickly. Actually that was when I learned to smoke.

It is difficult to sift one particular event out of so many memories. Some are longer, some are ornery, and some are ugly. In combat terms, I did not do as much as some, but more than others. It used to make me feel unworthy of participating in some events. I feel the same way about my Purple Heart. My wartime experience was a monumental change in my life. I turned 20 there. I felt like our press ruined us at home and I despise them today. They continue to harm those defending us still. Our government sent us to fight and then tied our hands, just like what is happening now. History teaches politicians nothing. They are so arrogant that they believe they can do the same thing over and over again with a different result. I am proud I served and would again.

I have served my community in a variety of service organizations. I was also a member of a local school board of trustees for sixteen years and established a local scholarship committee.

I am a believer in all that is good about the United States of America.

~ Michael D. Mullins, U.S. Army, Vietnam Veteran and author of *Out of the Mist, Memories of War*

> **"**
> The war left many of us changed. After the TET Offensive, I came home different and after 47 years I finally sought help.
> **"**
>
> ~ Vietnam Vet

DOMINICK FONDO

U.S. ARMY

"THE MACHINE GUN WON."

My name is Dominick Fondo but everyone calls me Nick.

I served in the U.S. Army from 1964 to 1968, in Ft. Jackson, S.C., Ft. Benning, Ga., Germany, South Vietnam, Japan, with the last year at Ft. Dix N.J.

I started in Germany with the 8th Mountain Infantry from 1964 to 1965. Then I joined the best unit of all, 101st 1/327th, Abn. Inf.

A Co. (known as Abu) and was with them during the last part of December 1965 through December 1966. I was hit at a place called Dak-To. I was a machine gunner 3rd Platoon Abu. The 502nd became surrounded and we were at a dead run through the jungle to relieve the pressure on them. We became encircled by the 24th NVA re-enforced regiment and were in battle for our lives. The battle lasted for about two weeks. I was hit the first night along with my assistant gunner, Lawrence Kalawe (Pineapple).

I believe Pete Griffin and I met the first or second night of battle. He was inserted along with about four other 502nd guys. He was one of the best troopers I ever had the pleasure of serving with. The chopper started taking heavy fire and had to leave. Pete and I were both in the Battle for Dak-To in 1966. It turned out that both Pete's brother and mine were in Korea together. We do not know if they knew each other. The first night all Pete and I did was load bodies on choppers.

My MOS was heavy weapons. When I first arrived in the Company I was assigned to a Sgt. Martinez as a rifleman. Soon thereafter, Sgt. Mitchell of the Weapons Squad asked if I would take over as a Machine Gunner. When I told him I was very happy where I was, his reply was, "Well you know weapons platoon is looking for someone to carry (Hump) the base plate for the 81mm Mortar!" Quick deduction, 80-90 lb. base plate vs. 12 lb. machine gun, the machine gun won. Sgt. Mitchell wrote a book called "Fate Unknown," which is a truly wonderful read about life as a grunt in Nam.

Four of my brothers served; Michael D. Fondo (deceased) Korea w/187th, then 1st Cav. who was wounded at Pork Chop, Frank E. Fondo of U.S. Navy Hard Hat School, Richard E. Fondo (deceased) U.S. Navy, and Ronald S. Fondo, U.S. Navy. Mike and I would speak of our wartime experiences.

Prior to Nam, I never so much as had a fight while growing up. But after Nam for many years, I became extremely angry and at times vicious if someone crossed me. Getting captured by the NVA was my greatest fear.

My return home was not a pleasant experience. One hippie made the mistake of calling me a baby killer. I went off on him and ended up in jail. He went to the hospital. Today, I am rated 100% with total and permanent disabled P.T.S.D. and 40% wounds.

My daughter is helping to produce a true, poignant and thought provoking video about suicide and survival. Together, she and her associates are trying to help save the lives of combat Veterans, or victims of bullying. She wants to help anyone in despair that is despondent, and needs a helping hand to walk with them through the darkness and gloom, of this life-threatening and indiscriminate, dismal state of possible, self-destruction.

No matter the cause, no matter what the stimuli, suicide is not the answer.

~ Nick Fondo, U.S. Army, Vietnam Veteran

> **"**
> It is appalling to hear about how poorly our Vietnam Veterans were, and still are being treated.
>
> These soldiers did what they had to do and we owe them for their service and for preserving America's freedoms.
> **"**
>
> ~ Patriot

CHARLES A. BURNHAM

U.S. ARMY

"NO THANK YOU FOR YOUR SACRIFICE OR SERVICE."

I have never really spoken about my experiences and tour in Vietnam, not until now.

I was with the U.S. Army, Joint Services of J-2 counterintelligence Directorate, as a Military Intelligence Coordinator. There are things that I have rarely spoken of since Vietnam. It is very emotional and difficult to re-live those experiences. Although I was never injured, I do suffer from the traumatic events witnessed and the emotions, which take over when talking about it. The war changed me, in respect to how I view people in the military and why they go to defend our country.

I had several fears during the war. The first was if my parents truly understood what I was experiencing and enduring while in Vietnam. Secondly, I often wondered if I would make it home alive. I reluctantly shared my reason behind the fear of not coming home with my daughter Carrie. When I finally did, she was in tears and shocked. While working in Saigon at Joint Services of J-2 Counterintelligence Directorate as a Military Intelligence Coordinator my group did NOT carry any weapons on their person and had NO access to any weapons to defend themselves. They were given specific instructions that they could NOT shoot until the enemy was climbing the walls and only then, if they could see the whites of their eyes.

As I was preparing to leave from Travis AFB on 23 May 1967, on route to Cam Ranh Bay, Vietnam, I was advised to pack and bring double quantities of items from the U.S., because they wouldn't be available in Vietnam. I was just one of over 525,000 troops serving in Vietnam during the "TET Offensive of 1968". Upon arrival we were subjected to the wrath of errant, misfit U.S. soldiers who were set on 'humiliating, degrading, and stealing', from all new soldiers arriving into Vietnam. From there I was sent to Saigon to await assignment to another unit. While waiting, I ran into another soldier and we began to talk. At the end of our conversation the Sgt gave his business card to me and said to have the Unit call when I arrived. After reality set in as to where I was to be stationed, I went into the Unit and pulled out the Sgt's business card and advised them to call. The soldier asked if this was to mean something. However, because the name and business card was given to me, the Unit had to call. Shortly after, the Unit requested that I report for duty. While working a counterintelligence operation regarding the black market, I saw photos of black market items. They were some of the very same items that were stolen from the incoming GI's and myself!

To this day, because of the mental trauma of hearing the mortar rounds, explosions, etc., I have never celebrated the 4th of July. I still experience flashbacks during the summer time when most people are celebrating our Independence Day. There were some gruesome moments endured while serving in Vietnam. One of my duties was to match up military records with the soldiers that were killed and being sent home in a body bag. I saw the bodies of our soldiers that had been severely mutilated, dismembered, and tortured. In one specific instance, I saw a soldier that had his genitals removed, shoved in his mouth and sewn shut. These are things that nobody should ever have to see. It's something that one can never forget. It is something that neither the general public nor family members should know about what happened to their loved ones.

As my tour was coming to an end, I learned that 100% of the soldiers in the unit that I was originally assigned to had been killed in action. My reception home was despicable. I arrived home after serving my country only to be 'spat' upon by our own U.S. citizens, with no welcome home, and no thank you for your sacrifice and service.

My daughter Carrie, shown in this photo with my granddaughter Kaia, has tried for 23 years to hear and learn, of my wartime experiences. She has indicated that the Vietnam War is not even discussed in the schools today. She has always expressed how grateful and thankful she is for all that I have given her, our family and our country. Carrie has empathy for all who served and who saw things that never should be done or seen by mankind. These memories are forever etched in their minds and will never be forgotten.

I am beyond grateful that I was a lucky to have come home alive.

~Charles A. Burnham, U.S. Army, Vietnam Veteran

" Your group of brave young men came home to fight the PTSD battle.

You did this all without backing from your people and help. You carried these things alone and when thanked today, accept it proudly. You did your job and have managed well for years without a homecoming and only a band-aide. I am the wife of a combat Veteran of Vietnam, and am very proud of all of you.

Thank you for your service and Welcome Home! "

~ Wife of a Vietnam Vet

BILL JENNINGS

U.S. ARMY

"WITHOUT HER, I WOULD NOT BE HERE TODAY."

My name is Bill Jennings, and I'm a Vietnam Veteran.

I enlisted on October 30,1966, at the Army base in Ft. Hamilton Brooklyn, New York, and received basic training (AIT), at Ft. Gordon, Georgia. My tour in Vietnam was from October 1968 to October 1969 with HHQ & B Trp 3/17 Air Cav. I spent my first six weeks in Vietnam with Headquarters and Headquarters

Troop 3/17th Air Cav., 1st Avn. Bde. Some people are just not made for HHQ, so I worked my way to the line with B Trp. 3/17th Air Cav., 1st Avn. Bde, and worked out of Dong Tam, Vietnam. My MOS was 05B20 (radio operator), but that didn't last long. My next MOS was 11D40 (Liaison Sgt.), which just meant that I was the go between for "U.S." and the "Grunts".

I was stationed out of Dian, but the military felt my talents were needed elsewhere and reassigned me. My next stop was a step up to the war. I was assigned to one of 3/17^{th's} line troops "Bravo Troop" in the Mekong Delta, working in support of the 9th Infantry and The Brown Water Navy. That is when my MOS was 11D40, Liaison Sgt. It sounded big and important to a 19 year-old kid from NYC. That is where I got my firsthand taste of war. Everyone is more or less armed and dangerous in the war zone. Some shoot at you, and you shoot back. I could deal with the incoming bullets. But the mortars and rockets were the worst for me. I was unable to shoot back, and in my mind, defenseless. I was always scared shitless during these attacks. When your "room" turns into this as shown in this picture, it gives you reason to pause, and check for holes. The question of how Vietnam changed my life is hard to answer. It changed my perspective on life as a whole. I see death in a different way, not as the end but as a beginning. I feel the hurt and physical pain of others. For a very long time I thought I was crazy. As I check the list of symptoms for PTSD, I recognized many. Fifty years later, I know realize that I am not crazy. I am not alone. I have endured many hard fights to get to this point in my life. I suppose I have Vietnam to thank for it all, good and bad.

It was and always will be my honor to be a Vietnam Veteran who served my country. I call myself a "Mutt", because I have every color on this earth flowing through my veins and am very proud of them all. However, in this walk through life, I have only been seen as a black man, but that's okay and part of who I am. That being said, when I travel the social media pages of veterans support pages and e-mails, I see very few faces of color. We are all a proud people. We are proud of our service to America, no matter what our color might be. I would like all Americans to know there are many men and women of color who have served this country proudly. I want you to understand that it is not just about race for me. It is about pride in who I am, and what I did for my country. People of color like to see their picture, and know America is thankful. We all need to feel the love.

Many of our returning Veterans are dealing with PTSD, and at times this is stressful. My way of dealing with it was to create a wood workshop, where my tool of choice is the scroll saw. A piece of plain wood can turn into a piece of art that will be here long after I'm gone. It also allows me to give back to the ones who mean the most to Veteran brothers, my sisters and me. I get a lot of requests for pieces with military themes in them, so it is a labor of love for me.

To every woman who stuck by her Vietnam Veteran, I say thank you from the bottom of my heart! Having gone through two marriages, I know that being married to us is not a life for the faint of heart. Loving us is rough, to say the least. You know PTSD first hand. God bless you ladies, and my wife of 20 years, Elizabeth. Without her, I would not be here today.

During each anniversary of 9/11/2001, I am often asked where I was when the planes hit the World Trade Center. It has been one memory that I tried to stay away from. As with Vietnam, I need to heal from that day. I was on the morning Staten Island Ferry and on my way to work. I heard that a plane hit the World Trade Tower on my Walkman radio. It was like Nam all over again! For the next 5 or 6 hours I did what I could to help those in need. During that time I watched in horror as both towers came down, praying that as many as possible got out.

When I arrived on the scene, it was everything Vietnam was and more, but this was happening in America! Yes I saw everything including the jumpers, bodies, fire and smoke. I guess because I wear my colors (VN Veterans) I looked military, and people flocked to me, asking for help and asking what they could do. When I arrived back on the Island there was a reporter waiting with his camera. I knew he was going to take my picture. I was a mess and covered in ash from head to toe. As he walked toward me I was going to wave him away, but something stopped me. I knew what a picture I would make, sending a message of the horror of what happened that day on our American shores. When I got home, Liz took one look at me and lost it. I really was a mess by that time. This old man struggles with Post Traumatic Stress that surfaced once again. It never really goes away.

I helped many people that day, and I hope the little I could do for them, let them know we are all in this together.

~ Bill Jennings, U.S. Army, Vietnam Veteran

"
    Our tour of duty in Vietnam was made a little more tolerable with the presence of Red Cross Donut Dollies.

They brought back a little bit of home connection to our base camps.

Their love and devotion for our Vietnam Veterans will always be remembered just like it was over four decades ago.
                                    "
                    ~ Vietnam Veteran

SUSAN "SUZI" BAIAMONTE CONKLIN

AMERICAN RED CROSS – DONUT DOLLIE

"THERE WERE TRAGIC THINGS WE WITNESSED."

My name is Carolyn Susan Baiamonte Conklin.

As one of the many men and women of the American Red Cross that served throughout Southeast Asia and the Pacific, in support of the United States Armed Forces during the Vietnam War, I am very proud to be the recipient of the Vietnam War Commemoration Certificate of Appreciation, as shown in this photo and taken at the American Red Cross headquarters in Washington, D.C. We volunteered to go overseas, often to combat zones, to support and boost the morale of our warriors while they defended our country's freedoms.

My two older brothers served, one in the Army and the other in the Navy. I was in grade school at the time. I was born in Greeley, Colorado in 1945. After graduating from the University of Colorado in June 1967, a sorority sister told me of the Red Cross enlisting women for SRAO, which stands for the Supplemental Recreation Activities Overseas. It was also advertised in the Denver Post. During the summer and fall, I pursued working with SRAO. My major was in journalism and I

wanted to be "Brenda Star". I wanted the adventure and wanted to travel to another country. I knew there was a war, but until I arrived did not understand the full scope of it.

The only training I received from the Red Cross was a two-week orientation in Washington, DC. I adapted to the transition easily. However, I arrived during TET 1968 in Saigon, which was a city under attack by the Viet Cong and NVA.

In every location there were rocket and mortar attacks. We flew daily to Thunder Positions, which were sites where the infantry and artillery camped. This was different from base camp, which

was more secure. On occasion we came under fire while at Thunder Positions. I was at Cam Ranh Bay from January 1968 to April 1968, Lei Khe from April 1968 to August 1968 and Da Nang from August 1968 to January 1969. In this picture there is a South Vietnamese soldier and American soldier in Lai Khe. They wanted a picture with their weapons and a round-eyed girl. We represented their wives and sweethearts that they left back home.

My personality has always been a 'glass half full'. Our job was to raise the morale of our soldiers. We smiled all the time. There were no 'Debbie Downers' allowed. No matter how bad it was, we had to keep the morale boosted at all times. The majority of my memories are good and I have some extremely funny ones from a Bob Hope show. They brought in men from the 1st Marine division for the show. It was a rainy day but the minute Bob Hope appeared on stage the sun came out. Ann Margaret was also appearing with the Gold Diggers. There was a time when I was in Lai Khe. I was taking out one of the new Donut Dollies to train and to show her around. We went to a remote airstrip and had a quick landing with a Chinook. We did not know that the airstrip had been overrun the night before. We started to do our programming with the Vietnamese on the airstrip playing games and giving out prizes. A General flying overhead wanted to know what the two "blue dots" on the ground were. When he realized that those blue dots were two Donut Dollies, he quickly landed and had his aide retrieve us back into the helicopter and whisked us away to safety.

Nothing was unbearable. I was able to cope with situations. The thing I hated most was the red clay soil that became packed in your hair. No amount of washing would get it out. There was no hot water so we had to take cold showers.

The two defining moments that have stayed with me are when we got lost on a remote airstrip and the 1968's Christmas in Da Nang event, with the 1st Marine Division at the DMZ.

Since we flew in helicopters almost daily, my greatest fear was being shot down in the jungle. As a Donut Dollie, there were tragic things we witnessed, like the countless number of body bags and the injured in hospitals. But I always looked on the positive side and pushed the negative to the back of my mind. Not for one moment do I have any regrets. I came back to protesters and soon discovered that they were naïve and not worth arguing with. If you haven't been there, just be quiet. I was in Denver, Colorado when the United States pulled out of Vietnam in March 1975, and felt it was the right thing to do. The country has come a long way since then. I returned to Vietnam in March 2015, and visited all of the places where I had been stationed. It gave me tremendous closure.

The friendships formed and camaraderie of service, resulted in many good friends made with fellow Donut Dollies. We have reunions that usually include nurses too. The wartime experience led to a 36-year career with the military. After I came back I taught school. But the Army contacted me and offered me a job in Europe, running recreation centers for our military. When I returned from Europe, I got a job with the USO in Denver and through them I made contact with Navy headquarters, and worked in Recreational Services at headquarters in Washington, D.C.

I am now retired and active with the American Red Cross Overseas Association (ARCOA), which includes all who served in military support from all wars. We still have Donut Dollies from WWII, two of which are 96 and 101 years old. I am also with the American Association University Women (AAUW), which supports women and family issues, especially education for women.

I am very interested in supporting women's education because every job and experience I have had depended on me having a college education.

~ Susan Baiamonte Conklin, Red Cross Donut Dollie

"
    One minute your buddy was there,
and your life and his depended upon one
another.

Then the day came for only one to return
home.

Still the heartache of loneliness and loss
has to affect you.

I pray all hearts be healed

"

~ Vietnam Vet

STEPHEN PAUL GREEN

U.S. NAVY SEABEE

"YOU COULD SAY THAT WE ARE A MILITARY FAMILY."

My Great Grandfather Joseph A. Tinder served with Robert E. Lee.

This photo is of myself at 19 during my deployment to Phu Bai and TET 1968. I served with the MCB-3 Seabees in Vietnam from August 1965 to late 1968. I made four trips to Vietnam with the Seabees, one of which was to Chu Lai in 1966. We built the base out on Rosemary's Point named Camp Miller.

I was not a Marine but a Seabee. We dressed like Marines but were the Navy's construction battalions for airports, roads, hospitals, bridges, etc.

My younger brother joined the Marines and served in Vietnam, and we were both in Vietnam at the same time in 1968. That didn't make Mom happy! My brother-in-law Russ Russell, also a Seabee, served in Vietnam 1968 and so did my other brother-in-law Wayne Goodwin, aboard ships as fleet sailors. My nephews have served in Navy fleets since the Gulf War. Photos of my brother and I are on the bottom left of the group photo. My nephews and their father, Rob Stevens, are also in this picture in the middle bottom row, which served in the Coast Guard. You could say that we are a 'military' kind of family.

In the evening hours of January 31,1968, MCB-3 was hit with rockets. After the 'all clear' came I noticed members of the Security Company were in an uproar. It seems Richard Blevins was telling everyone he felt he was going to get killed that night. To calm the situation, I told Blevins that if he felt that way to go find him self a place alone and to stay there for the rest of the night. The next morning on February 1st, Blevins came running up to me saying, "Hey Green I made it and I am flying home today". I responded with, "See all that worry last night was for nothing". A short time later around noontime, we were hit with rockets again. Richard Blevins was killed instantly. I went to the CP to inform the command of his death. I was ordered to go and remove his personal effects from his body. Richard lay there in the hot sun with his eyes wide open. As I knelt down, I began telling him how very sorry I was and started crying. Someone had to pull me up. This is the only photo I have of Richard.

But this is not the end of my story. In 2011, I came across a gal on our battalion web site looking for information on her brother's death. It was Leslie Blevins French. We made contact via e-mail, and I assured her that he had not suffered and was not alone. Leslie and I are friends on Facebook and she attended our reunion last September in San Antonio. Leslie and I are in the picture together. Her speech at the memorial service did not leave a dry eye in the room. Richard was our last loss of the Phu Bai deployment. In 2011, I began my healing, and now I'm a work in progress.

I will forever remember my Fallen Brothers and am making an honest attempt to loosen the grip of the sad memories of the Vietnam War.

~Stephen Paul Green, U.S. Navy, Seabees, Vietnam Veteran

> "I was spit on and called a murderer upon my return.
>
> I would go back in a 'New York' second to proudly serve my country again!"
>
> ~ Vietnam Vet

ANGELO V. "ZIP" ONEVELO

U.S. ARMY

"I AM NOW AT PEACE WITH MY PAST."

I was drafted on the first lottery having #31 in December 1969 and served with the United States Army Bravo Company, 2nd Platoon, 1/20 Infantry, 11th Brigade, 23d Infantry Division (Americal).

My MOS (11 Bravo) was light weapons infantry during my tour in Vietnam from 1970 to 1972. I was promoted to a Specialist 4th

Class and I carried an M-16 rifle. The 2d platoon was comprised of 3 squads with about 6 men in each squad. Each squad had a squad leader with several riflemen (M-16), a grenadier with either an M-72 grenade launcher or M-201 rifle, which combined an M-16 with a grenade launcher, and an M-60 machine gun. We were all responsible to carry out the mission of seeking and engaging the Viet Cong and or North Vietnamese Army. Our area of operation was the Song Ve Valley, a haven for the NVA. I initially arrived at Battalion Headquarters in Duc Pho with about 11 other fresh recruits. We were randomly chosen and assigned to different companies. I was assigned to Bravo. Several went to Alpha. Within 2 weeks all the men assigned to Alpha were killed when their unit was overrun on Easter Sunday, April 11, 1971. I have often felt guilt, and struggle with the 'why not me' syndrome.

Prior to leaving for Vietnam I was given a prayer by a very good friend to carry with me on my tour. It was given to him when he served 2 years prior. It is a prayer to St. Joseph. The prayer dates back to the 50th year of our Lord Jesus Christ and in 1505 it was sent from the Pope to Emperor Charles to protect him in battle. The original poem survived 2 tours and was given to a friend of mine, whose son, prior to his going to Iraq participated in Desert Storm. He was there when Saddam Hussein was captured.

After serving 1 month in the field, LT Tom Dolan recognized that I was struggling as a grunt. I had already received my Bachelor's Degree and had one year towards my Master's degree prior to being drafted. The company needed a clerk and LT Dolan convinced Top (the First Sergeant) to give me a chance. Tom Dolan is my guardian angel. He answered my prayers and saved my life.

I was uncomfortable with the separation from my family and friends. The constant uncertainty of not returning home alive or of returning home disabled, always hovered over me. I was afraid of never returning home and experiencing the fruits of life. In the end, I feel that my service experience made me a hard worker, able to work as a team with others and remain calm under pressure. I learned patience and to appreciate life.

Memories of the smell, heat, rain, c-rations, artillery, gun fire, chopper combat assaults, mosquitoes, life, death, good laughs, bad laughs, brothers, patrols, bunker guard, day loggers, night defensive positions, guard duty, etc., are tucked away to be forgotten. I sometimes recall them. I often received letters from my parents, sister, and friends. The first time my mother sent a care package she did not know there was a weight restriction. The package was returned to her. It broke her heart! I received a birthday cake in the mail from the sisters of a very good friend. By the time I received the cake it was all moldy. The canned frosting was consumed with no problem. That is now a funny memory.

I was fortunate to be discharged from service and upon returning state side was stationed at Fort Lewis, Washington. Within 2 weeks I was back in graduate school attending classes, finishing my Master's Degree. I purchased civilian clothes prior to departing Fort Lewis. As a result, I never experienced any negative reception while traveling. Obviously my family and friends were thrilled I was home. It was a great feeling. I never had time to unwind and started working immediately after finishing school. I left Vietnam via Tiger Airline early December 1972. I stopped in Japan prior to departing for the west coast of the United States. While over the Pacific Ocean off the coast of Washington, about 3 a.m., with the cabin lights off, the pilot spoke over the intercom and said, "Gentlemen, if you look out the left side of the aircraft, you will see the lights of the United States of America". At that moment I realized that I lived in a land that was very special. Recalling this still initiates goose bumps! Leaving Vietnam behind was easy. Time to reminisce was sparse because I had a life ahead of me with lots to accomplish.

It was about 9 years ago while surfing the net that I came across videos taken by John "Wolfie" Wolfe. Some of the video seemed scarily familiar. I tried to contact John but nothing materialized. I am the annual chairperson of the Town of Niagara Lions Club Memorial and Veterans Day ceremonies. Following the 2014 Memorial Day ceremony, I was talking to several of the Conrad Kania Detachment of the Marine Corps League Color Guard, when, I mentioned that I was a Vietnam Veteran with Bravo Company 1/20 Infantry. Before I could finish, a hand was placed on my shoulder asking me to repeat what I had just said. As I did, the individual turned around and displayed his shirt, which immortalized the names of all the members of Delta Company 1/20 Infantry who lost their lives while serving in Vietnam.

After the coincidental meeting, we realized we were in Vietnam at the same time, walking the same ground and area of operation. The individual was Tom "Doc" Tierney, medic for Delta Company. Doc began to tell me about the "Wolfie" videos taken by Delta company rifleman John Wolf. I immediately told him I had contacted "Wolfie" quite some time ago but the conversation ended after one e-mail exchange. Doc called "Wolfie" and told him about our meeting. "Wolfie" began sorting through one of his videos, to find the one that showed Delta Company on a combat assault relieving Bravo Company, which ended a 2-week mission. Low and behold "Wolfie" found me standing next to Al "Sweet Pea" Walton, with whom I was in the same squad in the 2d platoon.

I received an email from "Wolfie" sometime during November 2014 with a still photo from the video, listed below. The e-mail was titled, "Is this you?" Can you imagine what immediately went through my head? Everything about that part of my life started coming back. Since this chance encounter, I was propelled back in time. "Wolfie" contacted LT Tom Dolan (my platoon leader), telling him he found another of his soldiers. In March of 2014 my wife Mary and I attended a reunion in Columbia, South Carolina, with some of my fellow 2d Platoon brothers who have been found. The group picture of us is below. In 2011 LT Tom Dolan scripted a book about our 2d Platoon titled, The Mad Fragger and Me, Leading a Rifle Platoon Company in Vietnam, by Tom Dolan. During the reunion everyone exchanged copies of the book autographed by each other. We plan on getting together again in 2017. Tom "Doc" Tierney, John "Wolfie" Wolf and I, are now great friends who have shared an event very few people have experienced.

When I came home from Vietnam I put all of my feelings and experiences away. I never talked about them with family or friends. They also never asked me about them. I never thought I would be revisiting this part of my life. It has been a whirlwind since "Wolfie" found me. Being reunited with fellow brothers is very surreal. No one talked about combat experiences at the reunion. The general feeling was just being proud of our service. I am now at peace with my past. When the 2d platoon gathered in Columbia, SC this past March, we all agreed that we are very proud of our honorable service. We are a small percentage of the general population, part of very few, who has experienced Vietnam as grunts. It has only been in recent years that people have thanked me for my service. It makes me feel very proud. I have always felt a deep sense of loss for the families who lost a loved one in Vietnam. We must never forget their ultimate sacrifice.

Front left to right: Bob Swanson, Terry Schilling, Harold Weidner, Tom "Doc" Wright, and Angelo Onevelo. Back left to right: Wayne Wilson, Frank Korona, Paul Malonson, Randy Guill, Dave Cox, Roger Steward, and Tom Dolan

I was President of Ange's Scrap Iron and Metal, Inc. I am 68 years old and retired now. I am married to Mary and the proud father of 3 sons. I have 2 grandsons, and 1 granddaughter. I am an active member of the Town of Niagara Lions Club and have been for over 25 years. I maintain their Facebook page with lots of pictures and activities. I have directed a considerable part of my life to volunteering for the band room at St. Joseph's Collegiate Institute in Kenmore, New York. I also volunteer at St. John de LaSalle church for the Friday fish fries as the head fryer, and as the Eucharistic minister.

I enjoy playing golf and take Alto Saxophone music lessons.

~ Angelo "Zip" Onevelo, U.S. Army, Vietnam Veteran

> **"**   I had many friends die in Vietnam.

I was a protestor during the Vietnam War because I was tired of watching my friends come home in coffins or wounded in body and mind. I never protested against the military, but I did protest our involvement in the war.

Though I proudly remain a hippie, I have worked hard for Veteran's rights, volunteered at the USO and in Veteran's homes. **"**

~ Patriot

Neil Hansen

U.S. Navy

"Most people just looked at me and kept going."

My name is Neil Hansen, and I am a Vietnam Veteran.

I served with the United States Navy from 1970 to 1976 on the ship, USS OKLAHOMA CITY CLG-5, whose sister ship was the USS LITTLE ROCK CLG-4, in the military park in Buffalo.

It's always hard for me to put anything into words. Most of my memories are being on the gun line and giving much needed support to the men on land. It felt good being able to do that. My original position on the ship was working in the missile house (TALOS), but during gunfire support missions, my assignment was as a gun Captain in the 6" turret! My military life wasn't as great as those that fought 'in country'. I always felt and knew they deserved the credit for that conflict!

I never had it as bad as the guys that were "boots on the ground". I am proud of them for that! I guess my time over there was a piece of cake compared to those guys. I was just glad to have been able to help give them support from our ship. Knowing that we were sending Naval gunfire support to help them survive was a great feeling.

My worst and greatest fear was when we were being shot at by the NVA and not knowing if or when we would be hit. We did suffer shrapnel from some rounds exploding in the air. I know this isn't as serious as the guys on land, but at the time I was young and not sure what was happening. The service and wartime experience gave me a new perspective on life. I never knew if or when the next day was going to arrive. It gave me a whole new outlook toward others and made me appreciate everything that I had.

Serving on a NAVY ship wasn't all that bad. I had a few scares when we were being shot at by the North Vietnamese Army, while conducting Naval Gunfire Support for the troops on land. I believe serving in the military helped me understand the needs of others and how to help others. I have stayed in touch with a few of the guys I served with. It helps bring back the memories.

I had four of my brothers all serve in the US Army. Three of them served in the 50's and early 60's, and the other one served in the late 60's to early 70's. None of them were Vietnam Vets. While in service, most of my communications were through letters.

I never had a problem with not having a reception after coming home. Most people just looked at me and kept going!

Today, I work part time during the week and enjoy being a member of the American Legion and the Vietnam Veterans of America, Chapter 20.

~ Neil Hansen, U.S. Navy, Vietnam Veteran

" When I came home, we never made it to the airport. We had to get off the plane on the tarmac.

When I sat in the airport in uniform, a little boy with his mom next to me, said to his mother, "Look mom, a soldier". The mother took the kid and walked away. She went to the other side so she didn't have to sit next to me in uniform.

That hurt worse than if she had slapped me in the face. "

~ Vietnam Vet

CHARLIE SPIVEY

U.S. NAVY

"SAILING INTO SERVICE FROM ONE GENERATION TO ANOTHER."

My name is Charlie Spivey, and I am a Vietnam Veteran.

The Selective Service tried to draft me when I was in high school, but I flunked the physical. I got called up, and headed off to Basic Training, 6 days after graduating from high school. My first duty station was Cape Cod Canal, where I served from August 1965 to May 1966.

I was an engineer and worked down in the B-2 engine room with CGC Half Moon from 2/67 to 5/69. I essentially kept tabs on the temperature of the engines and other things, including the Reefer deck, where we had the fridges and freezers. I had to go down the shaft alleys and check the shaft bearings and make sure they weren't over heating, along with the stuffing boxes where the shaft went out of the hull. I was in a repair locker during GQ, and on a boarding team when we went to inspect boats for contraband. The long hours with 130 degrees were pretty bad. I have never liked being in dark places since, where I could not see the sunlight. I had one case where we had a deadline to get one of the mail engines back online and we worked around the clock for over 4 days in the heat. I only left to go to the bathroom and to eat. That was part of my office.

This picture was taken just off the coast of Vietnam in August 1967. The coast is to my left about a 1/4 of a mile. I was in the Coast Guard from June 14,1965 to May 22, 1969. Another picture shows one of our many Gunfire Support missions, probably In Song Ong Doc, and Area 9, getting more ammunition for that big gun. We went through a lot of that. One of the worst things was when my leading PO (Petty Officer), had put in for re-enlistment. He left the ship in Bermuda in July '68 and went back, with CG RON 1. He was KIA in March '69 after getting caught in an ambush when boarding some boats.

The Coast Guard Squadron 3 was multifaceted. We were all well armed, and that included 81mm mortars as well as a 5" 38 mount. We used that in support of ground forces and supplied gunfire support. In one case we were tasked with taking out a large bunker complex. We did many of these missions as well as boarding boats. Similar to what they were doing on the Ho Chi Minh trail, we were doing just off the coast. We were trying to stop the flow of arms and other supplies from the North to the South. It got dicey at times. There were some cutters in RON 3 that were fired upon. We also undertook "Normal" Coast Guard work on occasion. We had a Filipino tugboat pulling a string of barges. We got a call saying that one barge was taking on water and sinking and threatening to pull everything down with it. We got on scene and sent a crew over with cutting torches, and cut that barge free to sink. The Half Moon was 311' in length and about 41' at the beam. It had a crew of 160 officers and men. Fully loaded, we drew a maximum depth of 12' 4" and could operate close to shore in rivers that had enough room for us to turn around.

I had lots of family members that served in the military service. One uncle served in the Navy and was killed, when the ammunition ship he was on blew up in the South Pacific during WWII. There were four more uncles that were Navy Veterans from WWII. One re-enlisted and retired from the Army after WWII. One of my uncles retired from the Navy with another uncle that was career Army, and WIA on Pork Chop Hill during the Korean War and later WIA again in Vietnam with the 1sr Air Cav, Air Mobile. He was awarded the Bronze Star w/ V for Valor. My dad was a Navy Vet in WWII and served in the South Pacific Theater. It was pretty much understood that the males would enter the service. My mom worked in defense during the war as well. That is were she met my dad. He was overseeing the work having to do with aircraft parts. He was an Aviation Machinist mate. Dad would have made it his career, but contracted TB and was medically discharged. Both of my brothers were Navy. My cousin's husband was retired Air Force.

We got the Fireboat treatment when we entered the Harbor of N.Y. The American Legion Post on Staten Island had a dinner for us, which may have been partly for recruitment. I didn't have anybody to greet me when I arrived. I never had a problem until New Years Eve in '68. I was out in Times Square and in uniform and had a 'run-in' with a bunch of student protesters from one or more of the local universities. For the most part, they just kept it vocal with some spitting, but one decided he wanted to take it a bit further.

That didn't go well for him.

~Charlie Spivey, United States Navy, Vietnam Veteran

> "
> I wasn't even born yet when the war was going on, but I was born with thankfulness and knowing where my freedoms come from, and how they are preserved. "
>
> ~ Patriot

BRUCE HOFFMAN

U.S. MARINE CORPS

"IT WAS HARD TO RELATE TO PEOPLE I GREW UP WITH."

I was a Marine flying as a gunner on Huey gunships during the TET of 68.

I was born in East Chicago, Indiana, and lived in Hammond until my parents moved to Tampa, Florida when I was 8. I still have relatives there.

My father served in the Marine Corps during WWII. Growing up, a lot of my father's fellow Marines would visit. I heard all their stories. He was wounded twice, once in Okinawa and once in Peleliu. I remember when I was older and would kid him about being wounded on the 3rd day in Peleliu. I would ask, "How bad could it have been? You were only there for 3 days". When my father was wounded on Okinawa he was taken out on a stretcher. His best friend was Bo Bo who had taken a Japanese pistol off of an officer he had killed. He put the pistol under my father on the stretcher and told him, "I'm not going to make it, so this is yours". Well Bo Bo did live and when they would visit over the years, he always asked for it back in a kidding manner. My father wouldn't give it to him. I have it now.

Since Dad and my two cousins were Marines when I enlisted, I joined the Marines too. My worst experience was Marine Corps boot camp in the summer of 1964. I enlisted for 4 years, and was in the rear with the beer for 3 1/2 years. I kept trying to get into some kind of combat. Some would say I was lucky, but being a Marine I needed to prove my worth. I finally ended up in a helicopter squadron, where I flew as a gunner, my last 6 months. I was in a three-man operations shop in VMO-2, a Marine Corps, Huey gunship squadron. We were at Marble Mountain just east of Da Nang. I wouldn't trade it for anything. The three of us flew every other day. My gunnery Sergeant was wounded and airlifted to Japan. I was a Sergeant and my Corporal was killed when his chopper was shot down. His body was never recovered. I was never wounded. But every other day, I think about how it could have easily been me flying the days that they did. My greatest fear was that I would be afraid, but I overcame that. I've been asked if the war changed me, and I didn't think so at first. When I came home, it was hard to relate to the people I grew up with, so I was changed and different. I have stayed in touch with several people that I served with on www.popasmoke.com

I wasn't too happy about the war when I came home. I didn't pay much attention to the anti-war people and was never confronted. I would have gone ballistic if someone had spit on me like some of the stories I've heard. I was dating a nurse soon after I came home and one Saturday I went by her apartment. She was making an anti-war poster. I fired her after that.

I wrote a book called *And My Mother Danced with Chesty Puller,* to recall the good times, and at the end I wrote about being a gunner. Chesty Puller is a famous Marine Corps General, and my mother danced with him once. My website is www. mymarineyears.com

~Bruce Hoffman, USMC, Vietnam Veteran and author of *And My Mother Danced with Chesty Puller*

"
Going through fighting areas and surviving it, you now know death is alive.

Next mission comes and more soldiers show up in front of the Chaplain. Some don't make it back, and some Chaplains don't either.

War is hell.
"

~ Vietnam Veteran

JERRY THOMAS HART

U.S. ARMY

"WE CAN WIN THE WAR THAT BATTLES INSIDE US."

My name is Jerry Thomas Hart.

My father served with the U.S. Army from 1943 to 1945. He was a POW/MIA and was field commissioned as a Chaplain before capture. He wrote down his stories that my daughter printed a few years before he died. He was quite a Hero. His name was Thomas Joseph Hart.

I was in Nam from August 1968 to May 1969 with the Army 5th Infantry Division. I was a Chaplain's assistant to Chaplain Al Skinner, who passed away in 2013. One day we were driving a jeep, and a kid came up to the jeep and dropped a grenade through the window and into Chaplain Skinner's lap. Thankfully, we both managed to roll out of the jeep before it blew. Neither of us got injured. The picture is of myself with my M-14 just before I left for Nam in Colorado, with the 5th Infantry Division Mech.

It was May 1, 1969, and I thought, "Wow I'm going to get out of here in 15 days". Then fear came upon me. Almost everyone who gets 'short' makes mistakes and gets injured or killed. I survived two ambushes, the TET Offensive of Feb 1969, and the overrunning of base camp in Con Tien and Quang Tri. I wondered if I would make it to departure.

I actually did make it, and got on the plane to Ft. Lewis, Washington. They took every piece of military issue we had except for our 'greens.' They told us to travel in civilian clothes to go home. I was proud of my service and asked, "Why can't I wear the uniform?" They also said there are those who don't like what you did in Viet Nam and to travel in civilian clothes to be safe.

It was when I landed in St Louis that I understood. My country had turned anti-military and racist. I was hot!

So, I kept my mouth shut, and became invisible. My family was the only one who really knew who I was, along with a few close friends. They knew the evil that lurked inside my mind, which tormented me for years to come. My country rejected me and now I was being immobilized by my mind. I wondered if there was any hope. In the late 80's I found that hope. 'No one understands like Jesus', as the old song goes. With His help and use of natural remedies, I started to grow and put the past where it belongs.

My wife Carla and I married in 1971. I can still wear the uniform. I retired in 1997 with the rank of E7 - SFC and have dealt with my wartime experiences by talking openly about them through visits with schools around Veteran's Day. I have also visited psychology classes in high schools and discussed the affects of war and PTSD.

My wife and I formed Holistic Healing: Hope For Health (http://www.herbal-remedies-holistic-healing.com), for people in search of natural herbal remedies and we continue to help those in need.

My daughter Lydia D. Hart, published the book, *Restoring Acres*, about a Vietnam Veteran who understands the struggles of PTSD. When his horse DJ, befriends a Navy SEAL, the friendship among the three becomes a partnership. Together, with a team of other military and police Veterans, they face times of fun, tragedy, fear, and restoration in their lives.

Lydia is married to a 1Lt in the Arkansas Army National Guard. They have 4 horses and a dog. She served as a mounted police officer for 7 years. Our family puts God #1. Lydia dreams of 'Restoring Acres' as being a real place one day. We would like it to be a place for military, police and their families to find peace, healing, love and forgiveness. Horses and our Heroes can find healing, trust, worth and love. These are the things that only God can give.

We can win the war which battles inside us. We MUST win or die defeated.

"In his kindness God called you to share in his eternal glory by means of Christ Jesus.

So after you have suffered a little while, he will restore, support, and strengthen you, and he will place you on a firm foundation."

1 Peter 5:10 NLT

~ Jerry Hart, U.S. Army Assistant Chaplain, Vietnam Veteran

"
   I lost a very special, kind, and loyal Marine friend in that awful war.

I am so sorry for the kind of treatment all our troops received coming home from Vietnam.

God bless you and keep you, always.
"

~ Patriot

BARNEY THARP

U.S. ARMY

"THE LORD WAS OUR POINT MAN."

As an infantryman with the 9th Infantry Division from August 1968 until June 1969 in the Vietnam War, I was a part of over 200 combat missions during my tour of duty.

Each of these missions contained different levels of danger. Some were short and relatively safe. Some were more aggressive and deadly, that lasted for several days. For our combat soldiers it was 'just another day at the office'. But it certainly wasn't a 'nine to five' desk job. Many of our combat missions lasted several days and nights on the battlefields, under conditions that still haunt the minds of too many. These combat missions offered up many risks and afforded us few rewards. I truly believe the Lord was our point man.

On the longer missions, we were brought supplies by helicopters. The supplies were routinely the same. They would bring us more ammunition for our weapons, c-rations for our meals, and dry socks for our feet. Occasionally we would get a special treat like watermelon. The smiles were sincere. After being stripped of all of the basic comforts that most Americans take for granted, we felt special in receiving the watermelon treat. What an awesome band of brothers! This picture was taken in 1968 at our base camp in Rach Kien, Vietnam.

I advanced from fire team leader, to squad leader, to platoon Sergeant, and on numerous combat missions, was a platoon leader. Opportunities for advancement often came suddenly with combat casualties, end of tour rotations and other duty assignments. At full platoon strength we had 32 soldiers. We operated with 21 to 22 men the majority of my tour. My platoon was the 1st platoon of Alpha Company, 5th / 60th, 9th Infantry Division. The platoon leader position was supposed to be held by an officer. They would come and go for various reasons.

Pictured here, is our operational briefing, the night before a mission. Lt. Pinkston was our platoon leader at that time, and was discussing the details of the upcoming mission. If the mission was to be near the Parrot's Beak area or the Plain Of Reeds, we knew that it would be difficult and extremely dangerous. Pictured here are (L-R) SGT. Mike Murrell, 1LT. John Pinkston, SSG. Barney Tharp, SSG. Ed Reiser, and SSG. David Lockwood. I had 'The Lord Is My Point man' on my steel helmet cover.

March 8, 1969 symbolized the worst of times for our unit. We touched down on a LZ (Landing Zone), that afternoon and noticed that the target area was mostly open rice paddy fields. Adjusting to the terrain, our company commander opted to not move out in formation, as was our normal drill. Instead, we extended out 'on line' to cover a wider area. This formation covers more territory but turns every man into a 'point man' with more vulnerability to danger. As we moved cautiously across the rice paddy fields, we were on high alert for enemy presence. Suddenly there was a large explosion. We all froze and dropped to the ground. That single explosion was followed by the most frightful battle cry ever uttered, "Medic, Medic!". Our medic Spec 5 David "Doc" Tiffany and our Company Commander made their way to the point of concern. We saw Spec 4 Dan Ebbole standing nearby with his facial expression telling the whole, horrifying story.

There was no amount of training to prepare us for those tough moments. Our beloved Spec 4 Danny L. Hanson had been killed. It appeared that he stepped into a broken plane in the rice paddy dike, which detonated. This was not an anti-personnel mine but an anti-tank mine. The tremendous force of the explosion had ripped Danny's body into irretrievable parts. As we gathered his remains onto a poncho liner, there was little to identify Danny. We were able to see his infamous 'Red Devil' tattoo on part of his left arm. Our job was to respectfully remove Danny's remains from the battlefield and put them onto a Dust Off helicopter. We had to regroup and focus. We had to continue our mission. That is what soldiers do.

The Vietnam War was a life altering experience for me. No longer did I take the basic essentials in life for granted. Vietnam gave me a crash course in Humility 101. I humbly thanked God for the chance to live another day and to successfully survive another battle. It's amazing how wartime experiences can make one appreciate the most basic things in life, like life itself.

After returning home my personal ordeal with the Vietnam War was over physically, but not mentally. When I returned to 'The World' I had left the rice paddies and jungles behind, but the rice paddies and jungles had not left me behind. The nightmares of war were frequent, furious and vivid in my mind. My 'back to normal' life was not so normal. I knew it never would be again. I met and married a very kind and caring lady who has been my rock in the healing process. I have a beautiful farm with lots of hills and hollows and seem to be located near the gates of Heaven. This peaceful setting has provided excellent therapy in learning to cope with, and control my wartime nightmares and memories. We were scorned by society, but hailed a Hero at home.

Let the healing begin.

~Barney Tharp, United States Army, Vietnam Veteran

"
My brother carried a picture of a young man he trained, in his wallet until the day he died.

He came home but the young man didn't. This young man died in my brother's arms. Both were casualties of Vietnam. My brother made it home but not as the person who left. He passed away in 2008 of cancer from exposure to Agent Orange. He brought his demons home with him.

Never Forget, Never Forgotten.

"

~ Vietnam Veteran's sister

FORREST EDWARD MYERS

U.S. ARMY

"HELICOPTERS WERE BEING SHOT DOWN DAILY."

My name is Forrest Edward Myers.

I was drafted at the age of 19 and served in Burma during WWII as a Military Police Officer guarding the Burma Pass. I repaired helicopters during the Korean War and later flew Huey's on my first tour of Vietnam. I flew Sikorsky Sky Cranes during my second tour. In between wars, I served in Germany twice. My specialty was helicopter maintenance, as well as test pilot and heavy lift helicopter pilot, delivering items such as howitzers to the Marines up on the mountains and hillsides of Vietnam. The search and rescue was mostly for downed helicopters, but if a pilot or crewmember was there, we rescued them as well. When I was flying the 'Crane', most of my job entailed delivery of heavy equipment, like the pods that went underneath the cranes for both tours.

My great, great, great uncle was General Thomas Sumpter of the Revolutionary War. Great, great, grandfather served also. I have a multitude of ancestors and family members who served on both sides of the Civil War and ancestors who served in the War of 1812. My two younger brothers served in the Army and were stationed in Germany. The family history goes back to the 4th or 5th century.

I will be 90 years old next year, and can speak quite frankly about what happened during WWII, while in Burma, which was one of the most terrifying experiences there. Our patrol was in the back of a 'Deuce and a half' (large equipment or troop carrier truck, called that because of it's 2 and a half ton payload), when we heard a noise outside of the back of the truck. We peeked out of the canvas covering the back of the truck and saw a Black Panther cat rummaging around the camp. We all decided that we would just stay quiet and sit back there until the cat left, because none of us wanted to be his next meal.

The greatest fear was not coming home alive. I hated writing letters and would send the family recordings. My wife would load the tiny reels on the reel-to-reel recorder, so the kids could listen to them. In the background you could hear mortar fire, gunfire, and all kinds of activity with me making comments such as "Whew that was close." It was decided then that I would no longer do that because it worried my wife. Whenever there was an OD Green Ford LTD running around the neighborhood, she'd freeze in fear, afraid that it was someone coming to tell her that I was killed in action. It was like that until I came home.

My first tour in Vietnam was in An Khe was from 1965 to 1966 with Unit B Company 15th TC Aircraft Supply and Maintenance Battalion. My company, which supported the 1 lift Battalion, was support for the General's aircraft and rescued, downed helicopters. We would fly in and rig the helicopter up so a Chinook could come in and pick it up. My daughter Deb Myers McKay, tells me that the dad she knew prior to Vietnam was a different dad afterwards. I went back for my second tour about 18 months later. It was after that second tour they saw a change in me. When I first returned home, the kids were told not to make sudden noises and be a distance away from me when waking me up from a nap or something. I was rather 'jumpy.' I had a lot more buddies killed on the second tour than I did the first. Helicopter pilots were being shot down daily. The toughest war for me was the Vietnam War. I remember convincing a young crew chief to go to Fort Rucker to learn to fly helicopters. But I learned a few years later that fellow was shot down and died as a result of it. I never urged someone to do something again after that.

As my kids got older, they would try to ask me questions about the war, but instead of answering, I would just mail them copies of the award letters received during that situation. The award letters told of what I had done to achieve that award, and believe me, they were some hair-raising experiences.

My daughter has been trying to squeeze my war experiences out of me for years now, but when we would get to the Vietnam War, I would clam up and say I didn't want to go further. The second tour was in Da Nang in 1968 with the 478th Heavy Helicopters in the Maintenance Detachment. I was their commander and flew missions averaging between 800 to 900 hours, which was more than the test flying helicopters did. I remember one incident where another pilot and I took a crane to a Marine unit to either pick up or drop something off. There was live fire all around the place except from where we flew in. I was second seat on the mission, which I did on purpose. In this way I knew the men were taking care of my helicopter. The pilot of the Crane asked me how they needed to get out of there. I told him "Exactly the same way we came in". The pilot gave me a questionable look, and I said, "Did we get shot at coming in?". He said, "No". I said, "Well, guess which way we're going back out?". The next day another two pilots did the same mission, when they got ready to take off, I told them how to get in there and how to leave, but they didn't listen. The fuel cells on the helicopter, rear and one of the tail rotor blades, ended up getting shot off. The pilot got shot in the butt and was evacuated out. I always checked on my helicopters every night before turning in. They were my 'kids,' so to speak. I noticed that one helicopter was missing and the guys told me what happened. I woke up early the next morning and grabbed another pilot and took my LOH out, (those little helicopters with the bubble fronts like they used in MASH units), during Korea. I flew to where that Crane was, and repaired it. I couldn't get the Marines to give me fuel to put on the front tanks to get the Crane back because a Crane needs two pilots and I was flying solo. The Navy was there though and gave me all the fuel I wanted. They filled it up, I repaired the tail rotor, and I flew that Crane back to the base, alone, without a co-pilot. The other pilot took my LOH back. Later on that evening, one of the officers asked what I was going to do about the Crane that was shot down. I pointed at it and said, "You mean that one getting repaired over there?". Questions began surfacing and I had to confess that I had flown it back by myself. The Colonel came by and said he was not sure whether to court martial me, or put me in for the Distinguished Flying Cross. I asked him not to do anything at all.

After my second tour, even though dressed in civilian attire (the command's recommendation) I was spit on after landing in San Francisco, California. The reception home was the deciding factor for retiring from the Army in 1970, versus putting in a full 30 years before retiring. I had 26 years in when I retired. I believe we threw everything all away during the Vietnam War. We were restricted as to with what we could do, and it was partly due to the protestors.

My daughter Deb is pictured here with me. She has battled cancer and won, and now helps others in the military, law enforcement, emergency services and fire departments. She heard about an organization of motorcyclists that stood at funerals, invited by family members, to shield the family and friends from protesters at the worst time a family could be going through. They officially started in November of 2005. She joined the Patriot Guard Riders and became a Ride Captain, and moved up the ranks to Assistant State Captain for East Tennessee. It is a position she has proudly held for nearly 5 years and is now a flag bearer, the most honored job there is in the Patriot Guard Riders.

To this day I attend Veteran reunions with the units I served with in Vietnam. As their Commanding Officer, I was always concerned about their welfare and I still am.

~ Forrest Edward Myers, U.S. Army 478th Heavy Helicopter (Sky Cranes), WWII, Korean, and Vietnam Veteran

"

    Not everyone is ungrateful, though I can see why they might feel that way.

We know freedom is never free and we thank you for your service and welcome you back home. We know what you gave us. We also learned how you were treated when you came back. We are here for you.

You are my Heroes from one of the saddest wars

"

~ Patriot.

RICH WAYNE

U.S. ARMY

"MY GREATEST FEAR WAS NOT KNOWING WHAT TOMORROW WOULD BRING."

When I returned from my tour in Vietnam in July of 1966, I wore my uniform and was fighting more hippies than the Viet Cong.

I began my journey to Nam on a troop carrier, the Daniel I. Sultan, one of 3 troop ships with the 1st Inf. Div. After ten weeks of jungle training at Ft. Riley in Kansas, we were ready to ship to Vietnam. We went to the airport to board a four prop TWA plane in full gear. The Salvation Army passed out coffee and donuts while we waited. I can't say enough about them. They were awesome. It seemed like we never slept from that moment on. We boarded the plane and flew to Oakland, California. From there we boarded a troop carrier, the Daniel I. Sultan with 1,500 troops on it. We pushed off and went right under the Golden Gate Bridge. That was the start of the unknown and uncertainty. The only thing I could think of was, 'Will I ever see home again?'. After a few days, we found ourselves in a Typhoon. Now you have to imagine what it was like with all the rocking and rolling around on that ship. It was a mess and so was I. We were sick for days. It took us 22 days to get to Vietnam with a short stop at Subic Bay. I was with the U.S. Army, Co. C, 2nd Bn., 28th Inf., 1st Inf Div. and referred to as the Black Lions of Lai Khe. As an infantryman, you do everything. Nam changed me a whole bunch. I used to avoid fights, but not anymore.

There was a squad leader that I felt confident with since jungle training, back at Ft. Riley. Of course now we're in Nam. Sgt. Blair was the company CP and was coming back to our platoon area on line. There was still enough light to pick out a silhouette of who it was. As he got closer I told him to "HALT!". That was a typical challenge/password. I asked, "Who is there?". He said, "Sgt. Blair". I said, "Advance to be recognized!". When he got closer, I said, "HALT!" again. I gave him the challenge word. He was supposed to give me the password, which changed every day. He told me that he forgot it. I told him to get down into the front leaning, rest push-up position. I came within arms reach of him and got down in a squatting position. I had the M-14 pointing at him, took off the safety and said, "Shame on you Sgt. Blair. You should know better than that.". So I had a couple of chuckles over that. The next day in the chow line Sgt. Blair came up to me and shook my hand with a few choice words for me, but was laughing when he did that. That is a man that I have never refused, and always looked forward to going out with on an ambush patrol. I loved ambush patrols.

My greatest fear was not knowing what tomorrow would bring and so I lived for now. My response to the people that ask about my experiences is "Scared and Lucky!" The group photo is of Donut Dollies seeing us off to Loc Ninh in June 1966. The Donut Dollies gave me a reason to keep my spirits up and make it home because the American women are the most beautiful women in the world.

Even the Vietnamese women would try to copy the western look. But it just wasn't the same. They were very brave to do what they did. How many young ladies today would do what the Donut Dollies did then?

We were on another operation in "D" zone setting up a perimeter when some choppers came in with supplies. Some crazy person got off the chopper in a bright blue outfit. Then I noticed this person was walking our perimeter. The person happened to be Ann Margaret in a skintight outfit that left very little to the imagination. What a moral builder! Of course she was being escorted by a full bird Colonel that was right by her side. It was amazing that she would go into a combat area like that.

The photo with me standing with the Vietnamese kids was taken in Loc Ninh during 1966. It was one week before leaving Nam and a day before our big fight on June 11, 1966. I'm 6'4" and all of 176 lbs. I always joked about being so skinny, that all I had to do was turn sideways and avoid being hit in a fight. That is not the case today.

Most of my uncles served in WWII or Korea. I had an uncle that served in Korea, and I told him that he was my favorite uncle. I would ask my aunt if he was coming home everyday. None of my brothers served. They are older and didn't make the draft. My Uncle Herb served with the 1st Inf. Div. in Germany in WWII.

I am kind of disappointed with the lack of respect and appreciation from the younger generation for my time and the people serving now. I personally believe, that they should have never stopped the draft and that everybody should serve their country. But that is the way this country is handling things.

The kids today don't seem to care about what soldiers are doing for them.

~ Rich Wayne, United States Army, Vietnam Veteran

> **"**   I served with the 1st Infantry in 1967. I was with the 1st and 2nd infantry in Lai Khe.
>
> When I came home I flew from Fort Dix NJ, to Los Angles, CA., to pick up my sister and fly home to Utah.
>
> It was a mistake to wear my uniform at that airport in 1968. I was called a baby killer and spat at.
>
> It is still a bad memory. **"**
>
> ~ Vietnam Vet

JACK MCCABE

U.S. ARMY

"I CAME HOME AN ANGRY YOUNG MAN."

My name is Jack McCabe.

I joined the U.S. Army 2 days after I turned 18 in December 1969. I went active in January 1970 and was discharged 3 years later on 15 January 1973.

I was trained as a 35L20, Avionics Communications Repair. I really only did that for about 3 months. Then I served as a 'fill in' door gunner, truck driver and in supply. I served in Avel Central, Phu Loi from 1970 to 1972. I also served with the 388th Trans. Co., in Vung Tau during 1972.

My father was drafted into the Army in 1941 at the age of 26, before Pearl Harbor was attacked in World War II. He was drafted for 1 year but because of the war he wasn't discharged until 1946. He served for over 2 years in the Pacific. My older brother served in Vietnam with the Marines from 1969 to 1970. My brother came home a couple of months before I went over. Dad rarely spoke of the war, and just talked in generalities or humorous anecdotes. As he got older, he spoke more about his wartime experiences. When he developed dementia, he would rarely speak, but once in a while he would look at me with a wild look in his eyes, and tell me that we had to check the lines because the 'Japs' were coming.

In my family, college was not an option. You either went to work or joined the service. When I graduated from high school I worked in a factory and hated it. Two days after I turned 18, I joined the Army. A month later I was on my way. I was very apprehensive when I arrived 'in country' like everyone else. You got used to it and learned not to be afraid or worried until there was something to really worry about. This has helped me throughout my life. I don't fret about things that could happen. The worst part of the war for me was the realization that it was all a waste, including the death, pain and suffering. The politicians sold us out and the American people treated us poorly, and turned their back on us. I watched Saigon fall on black and white TV. That was the ultimate worst day ever.

I came out of the military feeling that I would never again have something to prove, either to myself or anyone else. I remember sitting in my parent's home watching the news as the North Vietnamese Army was overrunning South Vietnam. It was April 1975 and the South Vietnamese government was collapsing. I watched my old base at Phu Loi fall. Then Saigon fell. I became angry as I watched all of this unfold and began talking to the television in an angry and loud voice. My mother was standing in the next room and began crying softly. I put my hand on her shoulder and asked her what was wrong. She kept crying and through her tears, she said, "I just want to see you happy again." I quietly left the house and went for a walk to sort things out. I was confused and felt horrible that my mother was crying. I didn't think there was anything wrong with me. I didn't understand. I felt completely normal, but obviously I wasn't.

I came home an angry young man. I can't say exactly why or when it started. It just seemed to build up over time. I didn't realize how angry I was. My anger just simmered for years and years. I tried to get past it but I couldn't, and the anger stayed. I had a couple explosive and angry outbursts after my unit's reunion at 'The Wall' in 2012. It was time to seek help. I went to the VA and saw a psychologist. He asked me why I was there. I said, "I have been pissed off for the last 40 years and I don't want to go into the ground pissed off." I am still dealing with those issues. The picture is of me in Basic Training in February 1970. I was 18 years old. The other photo was taken while visiting my friend Joe Kaminski in New York during 1975. He died in 2011 from Agent Orange, may he rest in peace. We have about 30% of the Vietnam Veterans from my unit suffering from Agent Orange issues, while many more have died since their tour. The average age of those that have died is 55.

I came home twice. The first time was in 1971. I flew into Travis Air Force Base and then took a bus to Oakland Airport. There were protesters outside the gate. They had signs and spit on us and called us baby killers. I flew home and met my family. I felt like I was in another world. I never felt comfortable at home. I turned 20 while at home on leave. I couldn't get a beer in a bar. I was kicked out of bars even though they knew I was just home from Vietnam. I went back to Vietnam and felt more at home than I did in Chicago. When I came home the second time, I was in a bunker the night before I left. I flew home on Air Force cargo planes, and it took 3 days to get home. We blew an engine over the Pacific. I thought to myself, "I am going to die here over the Pacific after all I have been through!" But the fire was put out and we landed in Hawaii. I had to get on another flight. It took me a long time to get home.

Upon arrival in the U.S. the airlines requested we did not travel in uniform. That was like a slap in the face. No one in my family knew exactly when I was coming home. I arrived in Chicago and phoned my parents. No one was home. I phoned my brother. No one was home. I took a cab home and broke into my own house. Welcome home.

Today I am a realtor and slowly working towards retirement. I am a member of Veterans of Foreign Wars, the American Legion, the Vietnam Veterans of America and the USAA. I work with buyers from USAA and Navy Federal. I enjoy working with Veterans.

My avionics unit website is www.avelvietnam.com. Expressing the way we were treated when we came home has helped to relieve some of my anger.

I am writing a book called, *Coming Home From War*, about Veterans coming home and readjusting from the experiences of Vietnam.

~ Jack McCabe, U.S. Army, Vietnam Veteran

"
Such a dark period in our history.

Thank you to all who served amongst all the controversy, and to the many who were there, to help lift the morale.

"

~ Patriot

BYRON MCCALMAN

U.S. ARMY

"IN A PLACE WHERE ONLY SOLDIERS WALK."

My dad served in WWII and was stationed in Yakatac, Alaska for 5 years.

He was my hero and my best friend. His last words to me were "We did it.", meaning he and I were Vets. Glenn McCalman, my uncle and professional historian, lost a brother in WWII. I served in the US Army and was deployed to Vietnam. I was initially drafted, and then I went RA. I was on watch for three months with the 220th CATKILLERS in 1969, and was as an aerial observer and a forward fire controller. I called in artillery fire and air strikes, including B-52 Arc Strikes from Guam. I also worked closely with Cobra gunships.

Most of my flying was at night (mortar Watch), for the location of rocket and mortar fire from NVA/VC in the mountains. After the heavy monsoon rains in October 1969, they discontinued the mortar watch, and from that point on, I was Intel for S-2 at camp Eagle Strong. I traveled all over surveying gun positions to the ground, so that 'call-for-fire' was accurate.

I went to Iraq in the beginning of 2005 and stayed for three years as a private contractor. I eventually went to Basra, Iraq with the State Department as a contractor adviser. The 3 years in Iraq were good to observe. I saw the differences in the way things had changed and it gave me a whole new perspective. Were it not for war related injuries, I would still be in Basra, Iraq with the State Department. In 2008 I saw more damage than I saw in 1 year in Vietnam. 'Go Fast' jets flew 24/7 for 6 months, and were carrier based. Rockets went off every day for months until my Special Forces crew nailed them. I slept no more than 3 or 4 hours at night for 4 months.

Slowly over the years, I have learned that prayer is the best weapon there is. From the day I set foot in that country and until this very day, it's been God first in all things. God brought me back from Iraq to pray for this country and the Veterans Administration in 2008. I have had decades to address the issue of Vietnam through heartfelt understanding. It is with the fear of God that I do. As surely as soldiers walk, they know the decisions overtaking them in battle, which leave them no choice. That is war. That is what it is all about.

I pray that God's anointing will flow to soldiers and their loved ones who suffer the imprisonment of war.

~Byron McCalman, 101st Airborne, Vietnam & Iraq Veteran

> **"** Nam Vets fought a war that wasn't considered a war.
>
> They went where they were told and stayed as long as they were told. But what they don't know is that there were a lot of people who saw them as Heroes back then. Watching the protests made me very angry. You are the people who made a difference to me.
>
> I just wanted you guys to know that not everyone was against you. **"**
>
> ~ Patriot

JOHN SCHRANK

U.S. AIR FORCE

"WE WERE YOUNG AND FEARLESS."

My name is John Schrank, and I am a Vietnam Veteran.

My father was in WWII in France and Germany. He was in the Army and a T Sgt. who worked in the motor pool with munitions. He didn't talk about it. My wife's brother did two tours of duty in Vietnam as a helicopter pilot. After he retired, he worked for the Kennedy Center in Washington doing security work.

Dyna Corp offered him a position to go to Kabul Afghanistan. We didn't even know he was there. He was very distant. Before we knew it, my father-in-law in his eighties at the time, had two people at the door telling him that his son had been killed in Kabul Afghanistan. The building where he was giving a lecture was car bombed. He died instantly. We had to wait almost two weeks for his remains. We did not know about the dangerous runs he did in Vietnam or the many awards until after he died. There is nothing like seeing an older man, accept the United States flag at his son's funeral. His name was Robert James Bifano. My father-in-law was in the Navy, but I have no other details on him.

I served during 1966 and 1970. My deployment to Vietnam was as an Air Force Sgt. in Phan Rang from 1968 to 1969. In high school, I delivered newspapers from my 1964 Ford Falcon, fast back. After graduating, I enlisted at 18. We were young and fearless. The reality was, we were really scared when they were dropping mortars and rockets with things exploding, which had tracers with red and green flares. There was nothing we could do about it. My greatest fear was being attacked at night while working on the flight line.

I was a Sergeant at age 20, and I was really good at being a weapons specialist. It required responsibility for one's actions and to those under you. As a result of serving, I grew up real fast.

As far as a welcome home reception, I guess I missed the parade. I landed in California and remember protesters yelling. They were on the other side of the fence. I did not care what they were saying. I was just happy to be home. I did what my country asked with no regrets. It was now time to get on with my life. I got married in two months. Our wedding was on October 12,1969.

I came home for Linda who was waiting for me.

~John Schrank, USAF, Vietnam Veteran

"

Wish I could write something that would make a difference, but I can't.

My dad was a true American who died in a Veteran's hospital with little care and no honor.

Our country and the people who put thousands of others through the military experiences should be held accountable to care for them upon their return. The men and women that served our country and the people in it deserve better.

They need support and understanding and an undying appreciation for their sacrifices.

"

~ Patriot

RICHARD CHAN

U.S. NAVY

"I WAS SUBJECTED TO DISCRIMINATION."

My name is Richard Chan, and I am a Vietnam Veteran.

I served in the US Navy from 1968 to 1971. My deployment to Vietnam was from 1969 to 1970 at Naval Support Activity Saigon, Detachment Dong Tam. I was an Engineman, Petty Officer 3rd Class, while in Vietnam working on River Assault Craft maintenance. I was also assigned to harbor patrol for 3 months. I am only 19 years old in this picture, which was taken on the Song My Tho, the upper branch of the Mekong River in 1969. Dad and I never really talked about my time in Vietnam, but he told me a few stories. He was in the Army Air Corps during WWII.

The picture with my mom and dad is after the war and she is holding me as a baby. I had one uncle that served in Vietnam who was a pilot in the Air Force. There were four other relatives who served in the US Army in Germany. My dad was an excellent cook. He was drafted into the Army but he did not want to do that in the service. He somehow got into the Army Air Corps band playing the drums and was stationed in Miami Beach. He learned how to play the drums in China during his Kung Fu lessons and took advantage of it. He would drum out the beat of the exercises as well as participate himself in Kung Fu. After he got out, he eventually opened up a Chinese restaurant with my grandfather in Rockville Centre on Long Island. His Sergeant came to the restaurant about 10 years after my dad left the service. They stared at each other for a while, and realized they served together in the Army. They became very good friends, and he was one of the regular customers.

I was subjected to discrimination, being called a "gook" or VC and got into many fistfights. Some I won, and some I lost. On my very first day in Vietnam, the Master at Arms at the mess hall would not let me in and said that Vietnamese sailors had to come back at 2 PM. I told the Master at Arms to read what it said on my shirt. He apologized and let me in. Another time an Army Lt. would not let me in the Army PX and said it was for US soldiers only. I had to pull out my ID to show him I was US Navy. I was fuming to say the least. I had a Navy Captain say to me that I spoke English very well one time, when I had to deliver paperwork to the administration hooch. I told him that I was in his Navy and scooted out of there! You should have seen his jaw drop to the floor when I said that!

I got into a fight with a South Vietnamese sailor, who I almost knocked out after he kicked me. He picked up my loaded rifle, and I thought I was going to die at his hands when my friend broke his rifle butt across his face, and knocked him out again. We dragged him to the brig. The very next day, I got cornered by 7 South Vietnamese sailors who were his friends and backed me up to the showers, with them yelling at me for beating up their friend. They were going to get even. I got lucky, when 2 US sailors in the showers heard the commotion and asked if I needed help. The South Vietnamese sailors disbursed quickly. My lesson was never to walk around in Vietnam, without a weapon, no matter where I was! To this day, I am never without, at least a knife.

When it was time to come back to the states, we flew into San Francisco Airport in civilian clothing, so the protestors would not single us out. I never got spit on but did go through the heckling. The guys on my plane all took a vow to back each other up in case it happened to one of us. These were the same guys I flew to Vietnam and worked with, for a year. We had each other's 'backs'. Once I got home, it was totally different. My friends were glad I made it home in one piece. My mom was the happiest of all. She told me that one day, a gentleman in a suit rang the doorbell and handed her a letter. She almost fainted. The gentleman told her that the letter from me was delivered to his home in error, and he wanted to make sure she got it. I never had any problems in my hometown. Even in the bars, lots of guys bought me drinks welcoming me back home. I had a lot of my friends from high school also serve in Vietnam. All made it home, but not all in one piece. I felt very lucky to be one of the ones who physically made it home alive.

When the end of the war was announced to the public January 1, 1975, I was at a Neil Young concert in the 10th row. I was with a whole row of friends when Neil announced through the concert that the war was over. Everyone around me was jumping up and down but I couldn't get out of my seat. I had this strange feeling that floored me and I couldn't move until my girlfriend pulled me up for a big hug.

Watching Saigon fall on television made me pretty sad. I thought about all we did up to that point, and when the South Vietnamese forces lost it all, it made me very angry. I was angry for all our troops who never made it home, and all for a cause we abandoned.

I see a lot of similarities with the wars in Iraq and Afghanistan. Our troops in Vietnam and in the Persian Gulf had to fight our enemies under the 'Rules of Engagement'. Our enemies didn't have rules, nor did they observe the Geneva Convention. We have gutless politicians that send us to fight a war with our hands tied and then block the VA funding for taking care of Veterans afterwards.

My war experience has caused me a lot of anger, anxiety, and nightmares. I suffer from PTSD, and I am 100% service, related disabled. This is my wife, Louise and I. I keep busy as a DAV Dept. Service Officer to keep my PTSD symptoms to a minimum. The satisfaction that I get from helping my fellow Veterans has eased my pain and helped me to continue on. I am the Treasurer for Disabled American Veterans, Brooklyn Chapter 28. I am also part of Disabled American Veterans Dept. of NY, Dept. Service Officers. I help Veterans file their service-connected claims for disability.

I am also the Treasurer, Membership Chairman, Newsletter Editor and Website Editor for Vietnam Veterans of America Chapter 72.

~Richard Chan, U.S. Navy, Vietnam Veteran

> " Thank you for your service and for tolerating those who used their freedom of speech to hurt you, and others back then and now. "
>
> ~ Patriot

TOM HAINES

U.S. ARMY

"SNAFU, MY VIETNAM VACATION 1969."

My name is Tom Haines, and I am a Vietnam Veteran.

The scarf in this picture should have been turned down. But I wanted to see if I could still fit into my uniform, and I did. My basic and advanced infantry training was in Ft. Dix, New Jersey, from January into May of 1968 with an MOS 11B10. I went through officer candidate training for the 93rd Co., 9th Student Battalion, 3rd Platoon, which took place at Ft. Benning,

Georgia, in July and August of 1968. I dropped out of OCS and volunteered to train a scout dog to walk point in search and destroy missions. My dog was taken away before I got to meet him/ her and I was handed a typewriter and sent to supply school. It was discovered that I had a business degree, and I was given my new MOS, Supply Specialist, where I worked in the 26th IPSD from August 1968 to April 1969.

My next assignment was in Vietnam with the HHC 3/12 Infantry, 4th Infantry Division, CO's driver/supply from May 25, 1969 to November 14, 1969. The picture of me was taken in Pleiku. The group picture of the Montagnard children was taken somewhere in the Central Highlands of Vietnam in August of 1969. As a driver outside the base camp, I would see detours around a blown up bridge, burned out trucks rusting in a ditch, and forests leveled by Agent Orange; All reminders that I wasn't on a leisurely drive for a day at the beach.

My greatest fear was making a simple decision that would turn fatal. I came upon a little boy limping down a road and offered him a ride home. He directed me into an area I shouldn't have entered. A couple of minutes later the kid hit the floorboard with lightning speed, draped his arms over his head, and repeated the word "VC", over and over. My vision was blocked by what appeared to be a water buffalo in my path. I looked out my window and was face to face with a VC standing on the side of the road staring at me. My heart started beating so fast I could feel my shirt move. Thank God the 'cow' didn't linger. A second, simple, but stupid decision took place in An Khe. Robert Creech and I were returning from An Khe and to Pleiku. A couple of captured VC or NVA were "convinced" to divulge information that the next convoy heading to Pleiku was going to be ambushed. Robert and I decided that jumping convoy might not be a bad idea. We jumped anyway and regretted our decision. The convoy didn't get hit, but we did with one bullet in the right rear of my jeep. There were other incidents, that are worse but I won't talk about it.

I was later selected to be the 4th Division Cartoonist. However, I received an early out to go back to college at East Carolina

University, School of Art. I had only one cartoon published. Here is one of the many quickly drawn, unfinished "roughs." I experimented with different styles.

When I arrived at the Seattle-Tacoma airport terminal, I walked at 'time and a half' to my return flight back to the states, so that I wouldn't have to acknowledge stares and dirty-looks. I'd heard stories from a couple of my buddies about getting spit on, and was called names like baby killer and murderer. It was a strange, almost surreal trek, quickly glancing at businessmen, families, college students, and other soldiers that didn't appear to be aware of my existence. As it turned out, I actually got a thumb's up, from a hippie, before I got my one, dirty look. That one nasty stare came from another hippie wearing a three-piece suit. I wondered how he interpreted my return stare. His look was pretty innocuous considering that my imagination had me running through a gauntlet of hate and disgust, the length of the entire concourse.

The final leg of my journey half way around the world was out of Ft. Lauderdale, Fl., many hundreds of miles from my home in Endicott, NY. As luck would have it, my parents were on vacation in the Bahamas and that's where I would officially start my new life. I was the last to board the plane and took the only empty seat. Just as I got settled in, the Captain's voice came over the intercom with the usual greeting. "Ahhhhhhhh, welcome aboard flight 38 to the island of the Grand Bahamas, home of Freeport, Lucaya. Before I give you the times and temperatures, I would like to welcome on board a returning soldier from Vietnam." 'Uh oh, here come the spit balls,' I thought. He continued, "If no one objects I would like to invite this young man to first class." I flushed from head to toe as the air filled with applause. 'Damn', I thought. 'I don't remember getting the Medal of Honor'. But, hey, I wasn't going to argue. I headed to the front while receiving a couple of pats on the back. Now that was my kind of gauntlet!

I was a fence rider, also known as a 'Dawk', a combination of a dove and a hawk. I was not for, or against the war politically or morally. It didn't take me long to grow dove wings. I had a hard time with supporting a war that operated on the 'reason de jour', mode of political explanations. I also had a hard time with the U.S. not fighting the war to win it. I joined many thousands of Veterans in Washington DC on April 24, 1971, voicing my feelings, and committing myself to the philosophy of entering a war as the absolute last alternative to 'problem-solving'.

The war experience did change me. I still have PTSD and the effects of being exposed to Agent Orange. I'm just thankful I don't have either one as bad as others. With 22 suicides everyday, it is tragic and disturbing to say the least.

~Tom Haines, U. S. Army, Vietnam Veteran and author of *Snafu, My Vietnam Vacation 1969*

> " It came with a heavy price tag for the United States also.

January 31st, 1968 was the single deadliest day of the entire War.

The military was willing to pay that price; However, hometown America was not, and eventually we got out of Vietnam. "

~ Jim Markson, Vietnam Veteran

DALE THRONEBERRY

U.S. ARMY

"I WAS KNOWN AS SKY CHIEF 20."

My name is Dale Throneberry, and I am a Vietnam Veteran.

As an Aircraft Commander 8 and helicopter pilot, I was known as "Sky Chief 20," with the 195th Assault Helicopter Company, and was in Vietnam December 12, 1968 to December 11, 1969.

I think my greatest fear was the fear of the unknown. No one told you what to expect. After landing in Bien Hoa, Vietnam we rode on an old school bus to the 90th Replacement Company in Long Bien. It had heavy wire on all the windows and armed guards that looked like Rambo. As we rode through the village of Bien Hoa, it was already dark and there seemed to be flashing lights of all colors going around us. There were many people in the streets, mostly children and younger men and women, staring at us with anger in their eyes as we drove by. We never slowed down. One of the guards said that we owned the streets during the day and the Viet Cong owned them at night. When the rockets went off, you never knew where they were going to land. Sometimes we would sleep in the aircraft in case we had to evacuate and the Viet Cong would walk the rockets up and down the flight line. There I was hiding under a helicopter with 600lbs of JP-4 (jet fuel) on it. Have you ever tried to dig a hole in concrete to get away?

The worst incident was in October of 1969. I was flying in formation behind our Command and Control helicopter heading into Cambodia to drop off a LRRP team. They were hit by a rocket and exploded in mid-air. As they fell to the earth we made evasive maneuvers to avoid getting hit ourselves. We quickly went around to see if we could rescue them. There was smoke coming up from the jungle identifying where they had crashed. We attempted to go down through the hole they made in the jungle. As we got close enough, we could see them and their helicopter engulfed in flames. As the ship exploded a second time, we could see the two pilots slumped over the controls. I saw the crew chief reaching out to us before he disappeared into the fire. Six people died that day and we had to take the body bags back to our home base. They were all good-sized men, but the body bags were no longer than 3 feet because they had been burned so badly.

I made many landings at the Ton Son Nhut Air Base, the target of major, communist attacks during the 1968 TET Offensive. The attack began early on 30 January with greater severity than anyone had expected. When the communists attacked, much of the VNAF was on leave with their families during the lunar New Year.

An immediate recall was issued, and within 72 hours, 90 percent of the VNAF was on duty. The first enemy rounds that hit Tan Son Nhut Air Base struck approximately 02:00 on 30 January. The chapel on the base was a direct hit, early on. The base was under the command of Air Force Colonel Farley Peebles. I spent over 1,200 hours in the Huey. I am pictured here with my friend, Ray Schrader in 1969.

If not for the work of the United States Air Force 377th Security Police Squadron in the early hours of the attack, the entire base may have been in danger. Four USAF Security Policemen lost their lives at Bunker 051. It was those 4 and two other Combat

Security Police members who received the Silver Star for their valor. The Security Police, despite being outnumbered, with help from the United States Army Helicopter and ground units, killed nearly 1000 enemy combatants. The base was secured by American and ARVN/VNAF forces, by noon on January 31,1968.

Over the next three weeks, the VNAF flew over 1,300 strikes, bombing and strafing communist positions throughout South Vietnam.

I could not help but be changed by what I did and saw. Seeing human beings, young and old, blown to pieces is going to affect you. It explains a lot about why the WWII veterans didn't talk much about their experiences. I can certainly understand now. When I came home I initially bottled everything up. At least I thought I did. I was reckless in my behavior. I kept taking chances and thought I was invincible. I couldn't understand why some people died and I didn't. I still don't. I showed many of the traditional symptoms of PTSD, but denied it all for about 30 years. The war in Iraq brought it back for me, and I finally got the help I needed.

Today I feel relatively normal, depending on how you define normal. Vietnam was a much more important part of my life than I ever realized.

~ Dale Throneberry, U.S. Army, Vietnam Veteran and host for Veteran's Radio

> **"**
> You can take the Vet out of the war,
> but you can't take the war out of the Vet
> **"**
>
> ~ Vietnam Vet

PAUL MCAFEE

U.S. ARMY

"HONORED BY THE PAST, PROUD OF THE PRESENT AND FOCUSED ON THE FUTURE."

My name is Paul McAfee, and I am a Vietnam Veteran.

I served in Vietnam from January 1969 to January 1970 in Pleiku, Gia Lai Province, with the 18th Eng. Brig., 815th Eng. Battalion, HHC.

My father was an officer in the Navy, but did not serve in combat. I enlisted to avoid the draft. I was in college with a 1.2 average, which made me eligible for the draft. I enlisted one week before my draft notice arrival. I wanted more control over what happened to me, but in the end, the Army had control, and I spent an extra year in service. After the Army, I returned to the same college and graduated with honors, Phi Beta Kappa. I received my MBA in 1995. I am now working on a Ph.D. in education.

This is a picture of me with a Viet Cong Veteran from the Vietnam War and was taken in 2012. My military training was as a Radio Teletype Operator. I trained in Ft. Bragg, NC, Fort Jackson, SC, Ft. Gordon, GA, and Ft. Benning, Georgia.

In Vietnam, I served as both a Photographer 85B40 and a Communications Chief 31G40, although my primary role was in communications.

When I served in the 815th Engineer Battalion, HHC, I was on Engineer Hill. For one Month, I served in Company D. We were located at the remote rock quarry perimeter outside of

Pleiku, along the Ho Chi Minh Trail. These photos show my photography and communication work in progress. My greatest fear was never returning home. One element of PTSD is that memories are blocked. I have vague recollections of events, but cannot recall the details. The movie, The Deer Hunter had three main characters. One was destroyed physically. One was damaged mentally. And the third came home stronger. I came home stronger, and much more mature. But that was at a cost…

The following is a poem that I wrote while in Vietnam that was later published in Stars & Stripes:

ORANGE-BLUE SKY

Tangled with barbed wire
Watching the watcher
Orange-blue ground
Echoing the thoughts
Of loneliness and home
Started by the fog
Ended by the sunlight

Dreams that are
Jerked
Back to the business at hand

Staring from the
Spotted flame of the
Tracer rounds
To the pulsing yellow
Of flares' eyes

Rows and plains of
Lights
That can't stand to be

Alone
And so have people
Like us sitting up
With them all night

I continue to serve, in a different way. I have taught Vietnamese since 2012 for Keuka College, a small private college in Upstate New York. The group photograph, which is taken in 2012, is of the leadership students in Hanoi supporting a local orphanage. Keuka College, founded in 1890, is a spiritually centered college of liberal arts and practical learning. I have taught business degree courses to Vietnamese students in Hanoi and Saigon for Keuka College. More recently, I have also taught business courses for the State University of New York, University at Buffalo, and in Singapore and Buffalo, NY.

I plan to complete my Ph.D. dissertation research on Project-Based, Learning pedagogy at a Vietnamese university in the near future.

~Paul MacAfee, U.S. Army, Vietnam Veteran and teacher

"
   God bless you for telling these stories.

I have a close friend, who also served in Nam. To this day he does not talk about it. In reading your stories, it gives me some insight to what my Veteran friend has seen and been through.

Thank you for sharing and God bless you for your service. Welcome Home!
                                            "

~ Marsha Stone

KAMMY MCCLEERY

RED CROSS – DONUT DOLLIE

"WE WERE ARMED WITH ONLY SMILES."

There were 627 women who served as Donut Dollies in Vietnam from 1965 to 1972.

My name is Kammy McCleery and I was one of them. Since we were contracted to the military, we were under their control for housing and transportation. We had to go through local, regional, and national interviews and pass an FBI Secret clearance. Our unit directors had to work with them to get us out to the field units and anywhere else.

As Donut Dollies, we were young college graduates who served in the American Red Cross Supplemental Recreation Overseas program during the war. They were a touch of home, a caring smile, and morale boosters for troops overseas. I loved being in the field with the men. We were armed with only smiles on the front lines of Vietnam, bringing entertainment, a smiling face, and a reminder of home. Doing my job out in the field, during the last 8 months of my tour with the 199th LIB, gave me enough war experience, that the 199th LIB awarded me the CIB in the late 1980's.

Four Donut Dollies died in Vietnam. One died in a jeep accident. The jeep was being shot at and went flying over a bump, and she fell out. A soldier at Cu Chi, later determined to be paranoid schizophrenic, who heard voices, murdered and killed the second Donut Dollie. Ginny had been 'in country' only a few weeks. The Army gave him an honorable discharge and sent him home. He was finally institutionalized after murdering someone else here in the US. The third, Lucinda fell ill, was hospitalized, and died of Guillain-Barr disease before they were able to figure out what it was. The fourth one, Sharon Wesley, another Donut Dollie went on to do a tour with Special Services, and to work with the women caring for the 'Bui Doi' AmerAsian orphans, who had become her passion. She died in Operation Baby Lift. I am exceedingly disappointed that the ARC has not recognized her service by including her on the Vietnam Memorial plaque in the garden. I maintain that she would not have died in Operation Baby Lift had she not been a Donut Dollie. I was injured in a jeep accident, leaving knee prints in the dashboard and splitting my head open on the top of the windshield. I almost lost my right eye. Other Donut Dollies had similar experiences, so I'm not unique. I was brought into the 24th Evac on April Fool's Day, 1968 with a 2" gash in my forehead. I had an unexpected meeting with the metal edge at the top of the jeep's windshield. Luckily for me, the doctor in the ER turned out to be a plastic surgeon'. He had been drafted and had three weeks left 'in country. He had reworked the first stitching done by a Spec 5. In a couple of years it was barely visible!

One of my dad's favorite sayings was, "Make yourself useful as well as ornamental!". So, on this day as shown in the picture on Signal Mountain, I did just that. I saw Marines from the first week in August of 1967 to the 1st week of January 1968. For the entire month of October, we were outside Pleiku. We got to sing carols on the beach with a bunch of the guys and held hands in a circle. I also got to sing at the 1st Mar Div Midnight candlelight service. To help bring Christmas to those guys was incredible! It was the best Christmas ever. The Marines were determined to not be the first to "lose" a Donut Dollie.

Looking back and reminiscing over pictures, reminds me of why I went and why my life changed forever. It involved a price, which I was not aware of at the time. I have PTSD and exposure to Agent Orange, but it wouldn't have mattered. I made a promise to myself the afternoon that the Marine amputees told me, what it was like to see and talk with young American women, and what it meant to them. I was part of that unique, sometimes misunderstood, program that existed to help young men deal with their time in that 'galaxy far, far away'.

I served with the ARC 67-68 in three different areas that were heavily sprayed with Agent Orange. I continually struggle with PTSD and the effects from Agent Orange exposure but cannot convince my doctors that it's Agent Orange related. Unlike the Veterans who served in Nam, I do not have a DD-214. Since I am not a Veteran, my local Veteran Center won't allow me to participate in PTSD groups and of course, I do not qualify for VA help.

My son, Chris Malloy served in the U.S. Navy from 2000 to 2015 and went on 8 deployments to the Middle East. He is out now, due to fibromyalgia, an Agent Orange gift to me that I have passed on to him. I wish that I hadn't. He is the handsome sailor on the far left in this group photo. Unknowingly, I also passed on second hand PTSD to him until he got his own.

I was recently put in touch with the Tohidu Project to participate in a women's PTSD group, and that is a start.

~ Kammy McCleery, Rec Cross, Donut Dollie

"
On the plane carrying military personnel home to the states from Vietnam, the stewardesses began spraying around the soldiers when the plane had landed.

A stewardess explained that by law they had to spray to kill any bugs they may be carrying from Vietnam.

Everyone was breathing in the pesticide, including the stewardesses.

"

~ Vietnam Vet

STEVE JANKE

U.S. AIR FORCE

"IT WAS LIKE WE WERE NEVER APART."

I was stationed at Cam Ranh Air Base with the United Stats Air Force in Vietnam from 1970 to 1971.

It was my first duty station after nearly a year of training. I had three months of basic then Security Police School followed by Patrol Dog School and a Combat Preparedness course. My dog's name was Kobuc. Our responsibility was to detect enemy movement and alert the base. We usually had to follow our dog alerts alone. Sometimes it meant engaging with the enemy. We had to protect the working people on the base and the base resources.

My father and his two brothers were in WWII. Dad would answer my questions about the war, but it was like pulling teeth. During the war he searched for enemy subs in a Navy Blimp. The war changed me profoundly. I became a Christian and a follower of Christ. This led me to being a minister for the past forty years.

The effects of the war are with me today. I have PTS. The worst part for me came on May 23,1971. Kobuc alerted into the woods, and we walked into an enemy squad trying to attack our jet fuel storage tanks. They threw two satchel charges at us. They exploded and knocked us to the ground. We exchanged gunfire while taking a few rounds of rockets. It was over rather quickly. There were two other K-9 teams involved with me. The fear of danger existed every night of our year of duty.

The military had several thousand, specially trained dogs that were in Vietnam and were later euthanized upon America's withdrawal. Most of us didn't learn about their fate for twenty years. It was a sad day. They deserved better. We have been dedicating monuments to their memory around the country since then. The reason the government gave us for killing them was that they had some kind of disease. This was not the truth. The dogs were listed as equipment, and all equipment was left behind. America's withdrawal was fast and chaotic. Last year our K-9 group met in Plymouth, Mass, for a reunion after 43 years. It was like we were never apart. We plan to meet this year again.

I am proud of my service in an unpopular war. My wife and her parents met me at the airport. I still had two years on my four-year enlistment. After 30 days, my wife and I drove to Fairchild Air Force Base in Washington State, where I served out my term.

Most people were indifferent to my service. Many of my friends were treated terribly at the airports. I was lucky.

Below is an excerpt from a book of poems based on my wartime experience and published in *Poems From A Soldier.*

A Pool Of Blood

A pool of blood lay on the ground.
A pool of blood was all we found.
I saw his face
It was so young.
I saw his face.
He could not run.
A burst of lead came raining down.
A burst of lead into the ground.
I see your face sometimes at night.
I see your face a haunting sight.
The next day you were not found.
Just a pool of blood lay on the ground.

The Vietnam War deeply divided our nation during the 60's and early 70's. Our returning soldiers during America's longest war were treated shamefully in parts of the country. In time, the public has learned to separate the war and the warrior. As a result many veterans did not speak of their years away from home for a very long time, if ever. It took me 20 years to slowly tell people by way of poems, what it was like. At first they trickled out. Then the trickle turned into a flood through the years.

My book, Poems Of A Soldier, is also about the wonderful War Dogs of Vietnam. My sentry dog's name was Kobuc. Our Air Base was the largest in Vietnam. The Security Policemen were the first line of defense to protect the many bases in Vietnam.

I served at Cam Ranh Air Base with a great bunch of guys that made that long year, almost tolerable.

Most of the several thousand dogs that went to Vietnam never returned. My book tells their story.

~Steve Janke, USAF, Vietnam Veteran, Minister and Author of *Poems From a Soldier*

> " As a spouse of a Vietnam Vet, I know about the pain, the anger, the fears, and the anxiety.
>
> The difficulties of war will continue to haunt your memories.
>
> We can't erase those, however we can be grateful for the fight you fought for freedom of others, and for the fight you fought upon returning home. "
>
> ~ Vietnam Vet Spouse

RON NOMURA

U.S. ARMY

"MY FAMILY NEVER SPOKE OF THE WAR."

My name is Ron Nomura, and I am a Vietnam Veteran.

I served between 1968 and 1970 and was deployed to Vietnam from 1969 to 1970, with the 1st Air Cavalry Division (1st of the 5th). My MOS was 11C40 Mortars.

I remember the children running up to me asking if I was Vietnamese. I would give them something like candy and they would just take it and smile. I had 4 uncles that served in the Army during WWII. One was in the 442nd Regimental Combat Team and one was used as an interpreter in Japan. The rest of my family was put in the internment camps during WWII, which was a pretty awful deal that our government did to my family and others of Japanese descent. Not many people know the history of what happened to Japanese Americans during the war. My family never spoke of it after the war. I had one cousin who served in Vietnam like myself.

Although my greatest fear was not coming back home, the end of my service was sad for me. It meant I would be leaving my tour of duty and all the experiences, both good and bad, as well as all the people I met. I became quieter and reclusive after the war and just didn't talk about it. Perhaps being away from family and friends had an effect on me. I really didn't do much when I first returned home. I don't really have a lot to say in regards to my time in the service. I don't intend on being distant, but that's how I am in regards to my time in the service. I am unable to talk about my wartime experiences, which is part of the symptoms of PTSD.

My personal massage business is Healing Solution Massage (www.HealingSolutionsMassage.com). I also belong to the organization, Hands For Heroes (www.handsforheroes.net) that offers free massages to all of our Veterans.

I am dedicated to helping the elderly, Veterans, friends and every person that walks through my door.

~Ron Nomura, U.S. Army, Vietnam Veteran

"
  When you came home, PTSD was not recognized.

Many fell through the cracks. Thank you for the service you gave. I was married to a member of the 101st AB and he served in Vietnam.

He came home a stranger and I was helpless to do any thing.
"

~ Vietnam Widow

CHARLES GANT

U.S. ARMY

"HONOR AND DUTY IS ALL THAT I HAVE."

My name is Charles Gant, and I am a Vietnam Veteran.

I joined the Army one week after high school graduation. I enlisted so I could become an Airborne Combat Medic. I joined May 31, 1967. I turned 19, December 5, 1967, and I was in Vietnam one week later. The Army did not have to honor any contracts or my request to become an Airborne Combat medic, so my jump school class and I were Airborne Infantry. A hundred of us were sent to the 2/502nd Infantry Battalion. There were thirty-six of us that went to Alpha Company and the rest were spread throughout the battalion. We were called the Strike Force Widow Makers, thus the Widow Maker patch. The NVA and Viet Cong who were pretty much wiped out in the infamous 1968 TET Offensive, just took off their uniforms and put on black pajamas. They referred to us as the 'chicken men', since they did not know anything about Eagles on our 101st Airborne uniforms.

My first six months 'in country' were spent mostly out in the jungles and mountains doing what we called Search and Destroy operations. We did Heliborne assault after Heliborne assault, many of which involved going into 'hot' LZs. Other than the rare stand down, the only time I was out of the boonies was when I was recovering from being wounded, which happened twice. At that time, or my first six months with Alpha Company, I carried an M-79 grenade launcher, a sawed off twelve-gauge shotgun, as well as a 45-caliber Browning Automatic pistol. Our rucksacks were over a hundred pounds each. They dropped down to seventy-five pounds just before a resupply, which was every five or seven days. We rarely took prisoners alive, but we did when necessary.

The NVA feared the chicken men to the point that there was a bounty on our collective heads. We were actually very proud of that. Right at the end of May or early June, I was one of the 'old timers' transferred into the newly formed Delta Company. I guess being wounded twice and having been 'in country' six months, even though I was only 19, meant I was an 'old-timer'. I ended up becoming a point man, a position I held until I left country in December of 1968. Even though a point man's life expectancy was only seven seconds in an ambush or firefight, I was never wounded again.

My mother accidentally threw out all my military records and photographs from my service. The group picture was taken at the Memorial Day weekend after our wreath laying ceremony at the 101st Airborne Division Memorial in Arlington National Cemetery, back in 2003. From left to right is my best friend, Lawrence Z. Rives, Dennis Huserau, who has past away, Roger McCord with the beard, myself, and Stan Inzer. This was the first time we had seen one another since I left in December 1968.

I came down with some kind of nasty bug, which caused my temperature to go up to 107. I was fortunate that I was wounded during the battle for Hue City, because I was already in a hospital recovering. When I got sick, I was told that I would not have survived long enough to make it to a hospital, if I had been out in the jungle. I was unconscious for eight days, coming to twice; Once when I was placed in a bathtub filled with ice and water and the other time when I woke up long enough to realize that I was covered with a lot of blankets. As a result of the fever, I became sterilized, unable to have kids of my own. I did not find out for 30 years that I had contracted a rare kind of TB called Testicular Tuberculosis. I have always loved kids, children or grandchildren, but I don't have any.

A sorry shrink that worked for the Durham, North Carolina VA, kept telling me that my wife and I should not get back together, nor should she come down with me for counseling sessions. I finally managed to get transferred to the Salisbury VA. The doctors were shocked to see that he had given me such terrible advice. My ex-wife later told me that she had wanted me to come back, but by then it was too late. She has now remarried and I am still as much in love with her as when I met her for the very first time.

Do I have thoughts of suicide, as the VA seems to ask each time I deal with that horrible bureaucracy? Suicide has never been an option. I come from a large Southern Baptist family and was raised to believe that killing oneself is a cardinal sin. I have lost way too many friends as well as the 58,000 plus men and women who paid the supreme sacrifice whose names now appear on 'The Wall'. To consider suicide would be dishonoring their sacrifice, and that I will never do.

I finally became a paramedic, something I love to do. But I did not believe in PTSD. I just figured that not sleeping for three or four nights at a time, daily flashbacks and ongoing nightmares were just normal for having gone through a terrible year of fighting in the jungles and mountains of Vietnam. It was only in 2000 after going into a thirty-minute flashback, while on call, that I was finally diagnosed. I will not bore you with my survivor's guilt issues. Would I serve again? In a heartbeat! I love my country very much.

Honor and Duty is all that I have.

~Charles Gant, U.S. Army, 101st Airborne, Vietnam Veteran

"
I wish things would have been different for all Vietnam Veterans upon returning home.

I wish more would have made it home and those who struggle to this day were better cared for. Most of all, I am proud of each and every one of you.

My Heroes fought in Vietnam.
"

~ Patriot and mother of a Veteran

DOUGLAS G LE FEBVRE

U.S. ARMY

"THE WAR CHANGED ME."

My name is Douglas G Le Febvre, and I am a Vietnam Veteran.

I served with the U. S. Army, 334th AHC as a helicopter gunner in Vietnam during 1967 to 1968. The 334AHC was based out of Bien Hoa. However, we flew missions, cover missions, and firefly missions all through three\ four corps. We were attached primarily to the Fifth Special Forces GRP at DUC HOA, where we participated in clandestine missions on their behalf.

We were on a three-month TDY with them to NKP, Thailand, operating in and out of Laos, North Vietnam. The worst part was consistent fear of getting shot down, captured, mortared, and having ground attacks.

One memory I have that is immutable, was when I knew I killed an enemy combatant for the very first time. I was riding 'gunner' on an armed helicopter gun ship, and we were called to bring support to an element of "mike force", B-36, near the Cambodian border. The enemy combatants had ambushed 'Mike Force Friendlies', so we flew in low from East to West, and came on two sampans, loaded with enemy troops. We fired on them. I followed my M-60 rounds into a rear-seated soldier, and watched as the projectiles stitched him from waist to head. The explosion of the torso, immediately made me think I had done well. It was not until the adrenaline in me had subsided that my Judeo-Christian teachings hit my mind full force. I had a very smart senior NCO tell me that I would see and experience more of the same and that I had two choices; I could accept this as the business of combat, or go slowly crazy, thereby jeopardizing myself and my fellow troopers. I took his advice, compartmentalized the incident in my mind, saw more of the same over my tours, and carry images with me to this day.

My return home was rather anti climactic, I guess. I stayed in the service with the 82nd Airborne Division, with much of the public in an up-roar having passed me by until I retired in 1975. The war changed me, and resulted in an attempted suicide in 1989. I was diagnosed with PTSD in 1990. I later spent 18 months in a VA facility for Alcoholism and PTSD treatment. I still go to VA Outpatient for PTSD.

Dad served in the army during WWII with the 82nd Airborne Division. He participated in Normandy, Market Garden, and the

Battle of the Bulge. He made a career of the military and retired in 1975 as a Colonel. My dad only talked about his experiences one time, for about two hours, when we were attempting to bond, after a long-time alienation. I guess the discussion with him helped, as it seemed to clarify our experiences and bring closure, respectfully to both of us. Dad had a major stroke shortly following that, and put our relationship on a different track. My brother is a West Point graduate of 1972, and although he did not serve in combat, was part of teams that verified Soviet Missiles, following the SALT talks from 1975 to 1980. He retired as a Lt Colonel in 1992.

I spread my musical ability, through groups that need a drummer and attend various jam sessions in the Little Rock, Arkansas area, keeping my face and talent in view.

It's funny that playing helps with many of my 'demons'.

~ Douglas G. Le Febvre, U.S. Army, Vietnam Veteran and musician

"
    The worst thing was the way Soldiers were treated upon their return home.

This should never happen in America again. You just don't send young men into war and then ignore them or attack them upon returning home. They did what they were called to do.

If you don't agree with the war that is fine, but do not attack Soldiers.

"

~Patriot

Evan Francis

U.S. Army

"THE U.S. POLITICIANS QUIT THE WAR AND DESERTED OUR SOUTH VIETNAM ALLIES."

My name is Evan Francis, and I am a Vietnam Veteran.

My father served in the U.S. Army Air Corps, China-Burma Theater, during WWII.

My father spoke very little about his wartime experiences other than an occasional disparaging remark about Asian cuisine. Apparently it was his way of commenting on the negative effects of war. One uncle, my father's brother, served in the U.S. Army Artillery and was in the Battle of the Bulge. He never spoke of his wartime experience to me. Another uncle, my mother's brother, served in the U.S. Army Medical Corps as a medic, but did not see front line duty. He also never spoke of his wartime experiences.

In 1962 I enlisted in the U.S. Army 'Airborne-Unassigned'. I wanted to be a paratrooper. By enlisting 'unassigned' the U.S. Army recruiter seized the moment and designated me for AIT as a Light Weapons Infantryman at Ft Gordon, GA, after my Basic Combat Training at Ft Knox, KY. After AIT I went to Ft. Benning, GA for jump school, and after graduation to Ft Campbell, KY, with the 101st Airborne Division, the unit I had asked to be assigned to. Upon arriving at Ft Campbell, Post personnel saw that I had a high score in my military tests in the area of mechanics and with my aptitude decided that I would be a truck mechanic, assigning me to the 801st Maintenance Bn.

Upon arrival at the 801st they found that I could type, which at that time was a skill in short supply so they reassigned me as their Company Clerk, an MOS I performed for one year. From there I went on to U.S. Naval Justice School, in Newport, RI, by direction of the Ft. Campbell Staff Judge Advocate for court reporter's school, serving as a court reporter for General Courts Martial for the next year and a half. The Staff Judge Advocate, Col Reid Kennedy, felt that I was officer material, talked me into re-enlisting for three years and helped me gain entry to Infantry Officer Candidate School, Ft. Benning, GA. I knew at that time that upon graduation from Infantry OCS that I would be in Vietnam within six months after graduation and that is what happened.

1962 to 1965 - Enlisted, E-1 - 5, 101st Airborne Division, Ft Campbell, KY.

1965 to 1966 - Infantry Officer Candidate School, Ft Benning, GA

1966 to 1968 - Infantry Officer, 2LT - 1LT, 54th Mech Inf, Ft Knox, KY; A Co, 2nd Bn, 502nd Abn Inf, 1st Bde, 101st Abn Div, Republic of Vn; Basic Tng C.O., Ft Campbell, KY

The one memory that is heavy on my mind was the death of my Radio Telephone Operator (RTO), Sgt Leon Thornton. We developed a closeness born out of serving side-by-side, 25 out of 30 days a month, on search and destroy operations. Leon was at my side at all times with the radio at the ready. No matter what the situation, when I reached back for the radio hand set it was there. He was an invaluable asset to our platoon. When I left the position of platoon leader and was moved into the position of Executive Officer, Leon was moved to the position of RTO for the Company Commander and died shortly thereafter in combat. When he was medically evacked to the rear I was the one who was called to identity his body. It was late at night in monsoon season and I will never forget that night as I walked back to our company area shedding tears over a man I came to love as a brother.

As I served in the capacity of an infantryman I viewed combat casualties and/or destruction in three phases. The first phase, pre-contact, was the most difficult because I was mentally focusing on the 'what ifs' with the thought and concern of being responsible for the men in my platoon. I needed to lead them effectively and do my best to make sure they returned safely from the mission.

I found that entering into battle and anticipating events would create intimidating thoughts and significant anxiety. The second phase was the actual contact with the enemy where casualties and destruction occurred. In that phase, because of the urgency of the moment, military training took over. I did as I was effectively trained to do at the U.S. Army Infantry School, Ft, Benning, Georgia, with no real time to think about or dwell on the combat in process. The third phase was often the most difficult because I would deal with the results of the event, such as death and destruction. Because of exceptional training at the infantry school, I was conditioned to accept the destruction of combat. I knew full well that casualties would ensue, but I never take lightly the loss of life on both sides of the Forward Edge of the battle area.

My wartime experience made me more appreciative and thankful for those who have gone before us in service to our great nation, and my responsibility to do my share in service to our country. The greatest fear was losing a soldier under my command in combat. Being away from my wife and children was the worst part though. I came home by a military transport in September 1967, landing at Wright-Patterson AFB, Dayton, OH, and then going to the Dayton airport for a flight home.

I did not have any negative experiences at that time. However, during GI Bill education at a local college, and in civilian life after discharge in March 1968, I did have a few experiences where my being a Veteran and my service in RVN were not well received. In all these events I clearly voiced my pride in being a Veteran and having served in RVN where we did not lose the war but instead, U.S. politicians quit the war and deserted our South

Vietnam allies. I am the last one on the right with the 101st cap in front of the 101st Airborne Memorial.

Today I am semi-retired, working three days a week in the private sector, defending product claims for a plastics manufacturing company.

~ Evan Francis, U.S. Army, Vietnam Veteran

"
    I am a Vietnam Combat Vet who served with the 1st Infantry Division (Big Red One), 'in country', January 3, 1967.

We fight our war every day. WWII Vets are referred to as the Greatest Generation, and Iraq Vets are called Heroes. We Vietnam Vets are still not referred to as anything.

The way our nation and people have treated us seems like it will never change.
"

~ Vietnam Vet

DAVE BURT

U.S. ARMY

"PEOPLE TREATED ME LIKE A KILLER."

My name is Dave Burt, and I am a Vietnam Veteran.

I served with the 11th ACR, 3rd Squadron Aviation Platoon, from 1968 to 1970. I was a door gunner until November 1969, when I was transferred to I Troop, but still part of the 11th Cav. I became a Track Commander on an ACAV. On January 19, 1970, we were on patrol in the Quan Loi area. We were ambushed, and I was then hit and wounded by an RPG, which was used extensively during the Vietnam War. The RPG was a should-fired, anti-tank weapon system that fired rockets equipped with an explosive warhead. I was sent to an evacuation hospital and later sent home.

The one memory that haunts me the most is picking up the bodies of two of our pilots that had been shot down. They were completely burned in our chopper and their body fluids were being blown around. The smell and taste of it is with me every day. After all these years, I still struggle with nightmares and anger. I don't know how a person is supposed to deal with the destruction and death with the bodies of guys you tore apart. I relive it over and over again, one day at a time. It haunts my dreams. But I honor them by dealing with it and not forgetting them. I am in Vietnam every day.

My return home was not a good one. People treated me like a killer and said things like, "You should have been killed for the things you did." There was no welcome home except from family.

My dad served in the Navy right after WW11, and I had an uncle that served in the Army during WW11 and was wounded in the Battle of the Bulge. Dad never spoke of his wartime experiences but my uncle did a little. He had a very bad drinking problem and died when I was young. I'm guessing that it was from his war experiences. My son served with the USMC.

This is a picture of myself at age 19 and fearless. The other picture shows our makeshift office space inside the helicopter. I later felt something was missing and became a Deputy Sheriff until retiring in February of 2014.

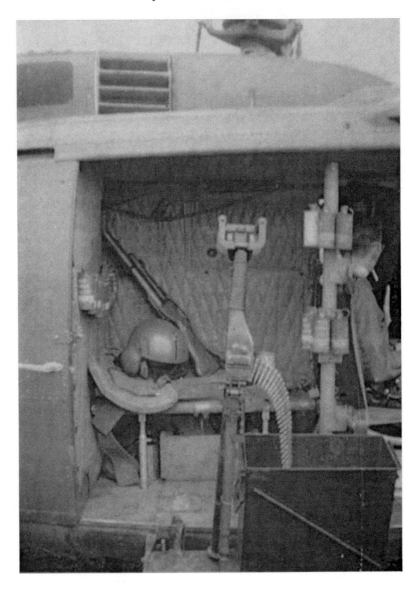

I love dogs. They give me calmness and undying love, which is what I need to help me get through it all. I love this country and would do whatever it takes to defend it.

We have our issues but I still feel we are the greatest Country.

~Dave Burt, U.S. Army, Vietnam Veteran

> **"** I am a 20-year Army Vet and I thank all my Vietnam brothers for welcoming me and all who have deployed in combat.
>
> You have led the way ensuring that no one will ever come home, without a hug and welcome home, ever again! **"**
>
> ~ Army Veteran

JOHN HUFFMAN

U.S. ARMY

"DEDICATED TO THE ONE I LOVE."

I was born in November 1946, in Hemphill, Texas.

I attended elementary school in Pineland, Texas, junior high and high school in Jasper, Texas, and graduated summa cum laude from Embry-Riddle Aeronautical University in Florida.

My grandfather served in the Army in WWI. My father served in WWII, and my uncle in Korea. All three were Purple Heart recipients. I was 17 years old when I joined the Army. I am pictured here with two classmates, and I was an honor graduate of the Fort Bliss Drill Instructor School.

I enlisted in the Army Airborne in 1966 and served two tours of combat in Vietnam. The first was as a private, and subsequently as a Sergeant, with Alpha Company, 1/27th Infantry, and 25th Infantry Division from 1966 to 1967. The second as an officer/aviator with the 120th Aviation Company, from 1972 to 1973, retiring as a Major in 1986 with three Purple Hearts, three Bronze Stars, sixteen Air Medals, one Army Commendation medal, two Vietnamese Cross of Gallantry medals, and various other service and campaign ribbons. I spent six years with the 101st Airborne, and seven years with the 82nd Airborne, both great units.

My worst experience was being wounded four times, for which I received three Purple Hearts. I was wounded twice in one battle, thirty-one hours apart, where I received only one Purple Heart for the two wounds. My greatest fear was when I was trapped in my burning helicopter and thought I was going to be burned alive. Luckily, I extracted myself from the wreckage and made it out safely. On another occasion, I took two pieces of shrapnel, one in my cheek and the other above my right eye, from exploding mortar rounds. This also resulted in the partial hearing loss in my right ear. The actual swishing and whistle of the mortars being dropped, was an eerie shrill and was immediately followed by an impacting explosion. It was virtually impossible to hear each other as they were coming in.

I was getting divorced and had a five-year old son. I thought I would never see him again because my ex-wife was moving from South Carolina to California, so I wrote a biography for him when he got older. Five years later, I remarried and my new bride found the manuscript that I had written, and had placed in an old shoebox. She read it and encouraged me to publish it. She encouraged all of the novels I have written subsequently, from stories I told her. All eight novels are dedicated to her and have won seven national awards.

Upon retiring from the Army, I launched a real estate, sales, and management company, bought and operated seven NASCAR speedways in five states, created an automobile racing and sanctioning body, (the American Racing Association), and developed three touring series.

When I returned from my two tours of combat, like those serving with me, I was spat on and called a baby-killer. My combat experiences changed me forever. I suffer from PTSD and am currently undergoing radiation and chemo treatment for cancer, the after effects of Agent Orange. I currently undergo five radiation treatments and one chemo treatment, a week and am half way through the treatment program with a 25% chance of success rate.

The following is an excerpt from one of my favorite poems:

"And sweetest in the gate is heard.
And sore must be the storm
That could bash the little bird
That kept so many warm"

~ Emily Dickenson

I reside in the Blue Ridge Mountains of North Carolina with my wife Misty. I have three grown sons and four grand daughters.

~John W. Huffman, U.S. Army, Vietnam Veteran and author
www.johnwhuffman.com

In Memory of John W. Huffman who passed away
October 26, 2015:

"The Next Place that I go won't be like any place I've been or dreamed of in the place I left behind. I will be free of the things that I held onto that were holding on to me. I take with me the love of those who loved me, the warmth of those who cared, the happiness and memories and magic that we shared. This light will shine forever in The Next Place that I go."

~ Warren Hanson, *The Next Place*

> **"** I did three tours in Nam back to back, and know that I was blessed.
>
> America will never know the real story of Vietnam Vets.
>
> Most of us can't tell the things that we saw without great pain. **"**
>
> ~ Nam Vet

FRANCIS EDWARD RENAUD

U.S. ARMY

"I FOUND THE CHEAPNESS OF LIFE PARTICULARLY TROUBLESOME."

My name is Francis Edward Renaud, and I am a Vietnam Veteran.

I am better known to all as Carmine G. I served with A Company, 2/502nd, PIR 101st Airborne Division. I also served with A Company, 1/505th PIR 82nd Airborne Division, and finished out my service with HQ and HQ Company, 19th Special Forces, 1st Special Forces Group (Airborne).

I served from 1965 to 1975. I served in Vietnam from 1966 to 1968 with a side trip to Africa that was a short-term direct-action mission.

While with the 101st I was a rifleman in a line platoon. While with the 82nd, I was operating with long range patrols at company and battalion level. I finished as a light weapons specialist, while cross-trained in operations and planning, while serving on an operational A-Team. However, I consider myself first and foremost a Screaming Eagle.

My father and his brother both served during WW II. My father landed in Normandy on 6 June 1944. My uncle was a gunner on a B-25 in the Army Air Corp. My father never spoke about his experiences except for the fact that he hated the German SS, and he had a great respect for the German 88. For the most part my father was an enigma to me. He was a supremely private person. You would never know what he was thinking or what his opinions were.

I enlisted in July of 1965. I knew I was going to be a paratrooper.
There was no second choice. I had to prove to myself that
I was good enough. I had already formed the opinion that
institutionalized learning was a waste of time. To answer what
was the worst part of the war for me, would take a couple of
chapters. I found the cheapness of life particularly troublesome. I

will touch on one incident about this. A very elderly Vietnamese, was executed by a recently commissioned West Point 2nd lieutenant. In his mind this man was guilty of aiding the enemy. The elder was made to stand in a rice paddy. The lieutenant shot him in the chest with his service pistol. Three things still remain with me; the stoic calmness of the victim, why I didn't do more to try to stop it, and the fact that I told the officer it was cold-blooded murder.

War changes everybody, just in different ways. I became pretty jaded. When I returned from my second tour I was told I was different. When I asked how, I couldn't get a real answer. I knew that I was just changed. Today I pray for the ones that I knew were lost. I also pray for the souls of the ones I took out personally. When you take a life, even in combat you change. No one can tell me otherwise.

What was my greatest fear? It would be, 'getting caught' and 'being taken prisoner'. I don't know what my metal, or how strong my fortitude would have been. When I got home I almost lost it. I hated civilians. Even the WWII Vets didn't like us. Everyone knows about LAX, getting spit on, yelled at and all the rhetoric. They threw eggs at me in New York. Until my last day I will never consider myself a civilian.

As of today, I still do not consider myself fully adjusted. I keep myself wired tight. I don't have dreams or anything like that. During idle moments the faces of the dead are always right in front of me.

Today I am semi-retired. I am a full patch member of the U.S. Military Vets MC. I ride with a NC chapter. This is a motorcycle club made up of Veterans. These are my brothers and we take care of each other. We cover each other's backs, just like in the military.

Being an American paratrooper is the greatest thing I could pass on as a legacy, if I may use it in those terms.

Ask any of us and we will tell you, 'We stand alone together'.

- Francis Renaud, U.S. Army, Vietnam Veteran

"
    I don't know where my patriotism comes from.

I think we are born with it. I use to stand in such awe of you guys that I could not bring myself to say thank you. I have grown out of that and thank you every chance I get. Don't be discouraged.

There may be others who stand in awe, but will soon be able to speak what they feel
"

~ Patriot

DOUGLAS GILLERT

U.S. MARINE CORPS AND U.S. ARMY

"FOR ME, THE INNER WAR HAS NEVER ENDED."

My name is Douglas Gillert, and I am a Vietnam Veteran.

I enlisted in the Marines while I was still in high school, mostly because I yearned for a broader life experience. I had never left the state of Michigan until I flew to San Diego for boot camp. I wanted to go to college downstate, probably at Michigan State University, but Dad said I'd have to go to the local junior college at least a year, and remain living with my parents. Instead I fled the coop. I served with the USMC from 1967 to 1971 and later the USAF from 1972 to 1991 and retired on December 31, 1991, with the rank of Senior Master Sergeant (E-8).

My father was a B-29 pilot, based in Saipan during WWII. My uncle was a fighter pilot in the European theater during WWII and another uncle served as a sailor and was twice sunk by Japanese torpedoes in the Western Pacific. My maternal grandfather served with the Army in Washington DC during WWI. My paternal grandfather was a sergeant major in the Army during WWI and was gassed in the trenches but survived with decreased emotional capacity. My future brother-in-law landed with the Marines at Chu Lai, Vietnam in 1965. My father, uncles, and maternal grandfather talked of their experiences. My dad shared with me books and magazines that depicted his service during WWII. My brother-in-law occasionally would share his experiences. I've never been able to share my experiences directly, but instead chose to write about them, often using fiction and poetry to tell my stories.

I was always a journalist in the military. I received no formal training but picked up the trade fairly easily. I had always enjoyed writing, and was self-trained in using 35mm cameras. I later used digital cameras to illustrate many of the stories I reported on. I was with HQ Bat. 1st Marine Division, in Da Nang, Vietnam from 1969 to 1970. The cruelty shown by Viet Cong and South Vietnamese, as well as by many of my fellow Marines was difficult for me to absorb and make any sense of. I think the constant tension of being caught up in actual battles hung over me, as it did all of us. We never could fully relax. I came to not be in fear, but conscious of potential doom all the time. I didn't want to experience extreme physical pain. Fortunately I was never physically wounded in battle, but the psychological wounds turned out to be a lot more difficult to live with. Feelings of impending demise stayed with me since my time in battle. I found it impossible to commit to lasting relationships or even fully commit to my work. By going back in the service I could cope with these feelings in the work place and had a highly successful military career. I was married and divorced three times and still struggle with a lack of true sense of peace and security. For me, the inner war has never ended.

I remember when we arrived at Long Beach. There were beautiful American women in bright sundresses waiting for our arrival. It turned out they were there to greet the sailors, not the Marines. We were escorted down a gangplank out of sight of the spectators, and bused unnoticed to Camp Pendleton. At home, it was subdued, and I felt no great sense of welcoming from anyone. Nobody wanted to talk about Vietnam. When I left the Marines and returned to Northern Michigan, there was no interest in my service from family or friends. After 18 months of marriage, even my new wife was disinterested in my war experience. I decided I would be happier back in uniform and joined the Air Force.

I became a correspondent again, covering the globe as a senior reporter with the Defense Department's, American Forces Press Service. Having been selected among this group of writers, along with the four years I spent as one of them, was the highlight of my career. The group photo is our crew and was taken on my last day at the American Forces Press Service in January 2000. Pictured left to right is Kathy Rhem, Jim Garamone, Linda Kosaryn, Doug Gillert and Rudy Williams. Mr. William is now deceased.

After leaving the press I got divorced, moved to Michigan with a new love interest and then to West Virginia. I got married again, moved some more, then separated and lived alone at the beach for a couple of years. I met a good woman, who perhaps is the only one who I've ever been able to share my experiences and feelings with completely. We live in the coastal mountains above Ventura CA with a large fenced yard, two dogs, a cat, and a pair of Sequoias soaring from our back yard.

I am more interested now in putting together the 'shared memoirs' of my combat experiences and others.

~ Douglas Gillert, USMC and USAF, Vietnam Veteran and author of *The Orchard Trail*

"
    I'm a Vietnam Vet and what is really appalling to me is how badly we were treated.

What is worse is the number of Vietnam Vets that took their own lives soon after returning home.

A lot of it has to do with the disrespect they endured!
"

~ Vietnam Vet

BILLIE TWO FEATHERS

U.S. ARMY

"I GOT WHERE I DIDN'T EVEN WANT TO KNOW NAMES OF NEW TROOPS."

My name is Billie Two Feathers, and I am a Vietnam Veteran.

I served with the U.S. Army Pathfinders, a 'ghost unit', whose primary mission was to infiltrate areas and set up parachute drop zones and helicopter landing zones for Airborne and Air Assault missions. The Pathfinders began in World War II when American paratrooper units needed a way to mark areas, and guide aircraft to a specific spot. This is my Pathfinder class picture, Pathfinder Class 2-68. I'm under the helmet in the back, just about dead center. We were told that we could wear what we wanted, as long as it was Government Issue (GI), so I donned that old steel pot. I couldn't afford one of my own, so I made a copy from a friend's picture that his son emailed me. That friend committed suicide exactly 20 years after enlisting. It's one of three pictures that I have of me in the military. My jump school picture was taken in July 1967.

The MOS was special, and they even censored my mail and monitored phone calls home, because of the security clearance. Did it make me better than others? No, I just had a different job than most. I was basically a glorified 'grunt'. I served two months with the 9th Infantry Division's Pathfinder Detachment. I was then transferred to the 1st Brigade, separate from the 101st, where I was embedded as a Pathfinder with the 2/502nd Infantry Battalion, 'Widow Makers'. I sometimes wear the Cav hat to recognize that time in the 82nd after I made Corporal for the second time. While with the 17th Cav, Vets from Nam were used to help train Cav Scouts that hadn't been to Nam yet.

I saw Vietnam from the Mekong Deltas to A Shau Valley and both western suburbs. Both divisions were busy doing what was needed at the time (1967-1968). Yes, I even met some old friends from the 9th Infantry when they replaced us in Cholon during the TET Offensive of 1968, also called the Battle of Saigon by some. I lead a company recon squad for a while, right after the 101st went Airmobile in 1968. After returning to the states, I was assigned to the 82nd Airborne Division, where I attended Raider School (Recondo), and enjoyed a few weeks of vacation at Ft Greeley, AK for Northern Warfare Training. I was discharged in February of 1970.

I was one of the lucky ones. I have several friends with their names etched into 'The Wall'. I was also fortunate enough to serve with some of the best soldiers in the Army's history. I am still trying to come to grips with a lot that I saw and experienced while in Vietnam. As the saying goes, "PTSD; Don't leave Vietnam without it".

My best friend from the 101st died screaming for me, and I knew if I had gone to calm him that we would probably be overrun. Hanoi had bounties on all of us. I always know when the anniversary of that terrible night approaches, even without looking at the calendar. He and four others died that night.

You would think after all of these years that I'd be used to it. Nope. It returns about a week before and runs for about 2 weeks. That's the cost of getting close to people during a war. We took so many casualties that summer that I was told it totaled a complete Battalion changeover, with the dead and wounded. I got where I didn't even want to know names of new troops.

My major accomplishment of my tour in Nam was finding out that the entire recon squad I had handpicked, all came back alive. I have to say that without Wayne 'Sneezy' Snyder saving my life the day before we took FSB Bastogne, I wouldn't be here. I had run out of ammo and saw an NVA working his way towards me. 'Sneezy' came over and sent that NVA on to his next incarnation.

My return to the states was typical of several people I've talked to. Family and friends would say, "'Been a while.", and leave it at that. Others would call me names that I won't repeat. At one job interview after discharge, when I applied to the biggest security company in the country at the time, I was asked 'off the record', if anyone I knew, myself included, had committed war crimes. I calmly looked him in the eye with that 1000-meter stare, picked up the application and told him, "I don't think you need this." That's when I tore the application into confetti and dropped it all over his desk and him. I did an about face and proudly left.

Like many, I have changed over the years. I quit lying about who I truly was and came out as a woman in 1998.

~ Billie Two Feathers, U.S. Army, Vietnam Veteran

"
    My dad was a gunner and he served 3 tours.

I am sad about the torment the Nam Vets had to endure because as a child of a Vietnam Vet, there were times they were my demons too.

You have my deepest gratitude

"

~ Vietnam Vet daughter

KENNETH BISBEE

U.S. ARMY

"NO ONE SEEMED TO NOTICE."

My name is Kenneth Bisbee Sp/5, U.S. Army, and I am a Vietnam Veteran.

I enlisted in the Army through some perverted patriotic sense, and with my people having been in America's wars since the Revolution, I felt it was just my turn to go. I was a helicopter mechanic in Germany for 9 months from 1968 to 1969 and later transferred to Vietnam in 1969. I spent 9 months in Dong Ba

Thin (near Cam Ranh Bay), and later transferred to Phu Bai for another 9 months. I was a crew chief on a UH-1H Huey with Avn. Sec, HHC, 18th Engr. Bgd. We were a small aviation unit attached to the 45th Combat Engineers, and did all the recon work for roads, bridges, LZ's, firebases, etc. We also flew paperwork to all the engineer places in I Corp and some of II Corp.

My father was on the aircraft carrier Shangri-La during WWII. He never talked much about the war, and he had issues with it that I never understood until I came back from Vietnam. My older brother, Ross, was in Military Intelligence at Nha Trang at the same time I was in Nam. What bothered me most about Nam was the stress and anticipation. We would fly over jungles from the DMZ, the Ashau, and down to II Corp. Since we were a recon-helicopter, we flew alone all the time and got shot at a lot. But the stress was in the 10 to 12 hours a day waiting to get shot at. The only General killed in the Vietnam War was when one of our choppers was shot down flying alone. My biggest fear in Nam was getting killed and being left there to rot. Flying alone just made the problem worse.

The worst incident that I remember was when I was on a little land-clearing base north of Chu Lai. The combat engineers were building an LZ and were under constant attack by NVA. It had been under siege for more than two weeks. We stopped in Chu Lai, collecting mail, medication, food and ammunition, and proceeded to the land clearing with a fully topped off Huey. The fighting was heavy and continuous. We called artillery to stop firing, so we could land inside the compound. We kept the engine revved up so we could take off instantly. A dump truck was burning next to us after being hit. Whoever hit the dump truck was still out there. The soldiers came running up to our Huey and started unloading the supplies, all while under rifle and machine gun fire. There was a field of five-foot elephant grass in front of me. We were instructed to shoot if we saw any movement. I thought, "The NVA knows where the helicopter is, I don't know where he is'. I put one hand on the machine gun, and with the other hand pulled down my harness. I locked it into the safety belt so if the helicopter took off it would take me with it! After everything was unloaded, the engineers threw a body bag on the floor. We took off with every NVA in the area shooting at us. Bullets were flying everywhere. When we landed back at base that evening, my door gunner and I inspected every inch of the ship. We never took a single round to the helicopter. All that shooting and the enemy never hit us once.

Vietnam changed me profoundly. I wanted to go to war and experience the things that my father and uncles did in WWII. I witnessed a lot of killing, death, and anguish during my 1½ tours in Vietnam. When I started flying, I was excited with new adventures ahead. But after seeing a small airbase completely wiped out and hundreds of people killed (NVA and ARVN), this dark cloud of doom settled in over me. I knew that I was not going to get out of this alive. I felt this way for about six months. Anxiety and anger were constant companions; Anxiety not knowing when I might be killed and anger over the senseless loss of life.

I was a stick-in-the-mud kid from Wyoming, always joking and kidding around. After I got back to the 'real world', I had problems with Agent Orange, PTSD, and anger. I was no longer the goofy kid who went to Nam, but an old man without a sense of humor, and little toleration for other people. I am still that way. When I got back to my hometown no one seemed to notice that I had been away, nor did they care. They all had real problems to deal with.

After I married, I settled down and became a good husband and father. My wife and I raised six children. Although I reintegrated back into society, the war will never be over for me. I stop in my tracks when I hear helicopters flying overhead and I cannot listen to Vietnamese being spoken. I maintain counseling for PTSD, and have a high PSA count due to Agent Orange, which may kill me yet. My children have all suffered from Agent Orange related issues.

After Nam I worked at approximately 100 or more jobs. The longest job I held was 4 years. Some jobs only lasted several weeks with my anger issues and PTSD. Because I didn't know what it was then, I continually searched in the job market. I mostly worked as an industrial mechanic, and for about the last 12 years I worked drilling rigs in the oilfield.

My wife died and I decided not to work for the man anymore. It's been two years now, and I still have a big empty spot. Lila was a huge part of my life. I was honored that she chose me to be her lifelong companion. She was the strongest, bravest person I ever knew. She had wisdom beyond most. Lila was the best mother and wife anyone could ever want. She loved her children fiercely, and all the other children in the neighborhood. She was the best part of me. She visits me when she isn't busy guiding her children. But I wish she were physically with me.

I miss her a lot.

~Kenneth Bisbee, U.S. Army, Vietnam Veteran

"   For some Vets like my husband, the memories never go away.

He is on constant vigil with lack of sleep. Some people can talk about Nam but many can't. For some, it doesn't matter how many pills are taken. Counseling or talking about it helps. Vietnam is still in their lives every night and day of the year and it just can't be eradicated. I know. I talk from experience and from being with my husband for 38 years and knowing him for 43 years. It breaks my heart that my husband and others can't find peace at night, not even in their sleep.

There are no magic pills or words to remove Vietnam from their memories and to make them better. "

~ Vietnam Veteran's wife

GLEN MURDOCK

U.S. AIR FORCE

"I GUESS IT'S ALL HISTORY NOW."

My grandfather was in WWI. My dad was in the Canadian Army during WWII, and my mom was in the British Air Force. I had 2 uncles in the Army During WWII.

I was in USAF from 1966 to 1989. I was military police for my first 4 years and then cross-trained into a C-141 Loadmaster. I was stationed as military police at Eglin AFB, Florida, from 1966 to 1967, NKP, Thailand, from 1967 to 1968, Plattsburg

AFB in New York 1968 to 1969, and then cross-trained to Aircraft Loadmaster. I was assigned to the 76th Military Airlift Squadron from 1970 to 1979. Then I was assigned to the 443rd Technical Training Squadron as an instructor for airdrop of personnel and cargo in 1982. I was assigned to the 20th Military Airlift Squadron from where I retired in 1989. Both the flying squadrons were in Charleston AFB, South Carolina and the training squadron was at Altus AFB, Oklahoma.

I enlisted because the draft was coming, and I wanted a choice of assignment. It most certainly changed me. It taught me to live for today because tomorrow might be over. The war changed me and the way I perceive people. I don't think my personality changed afterwards. I have a lot of good memories and lot of bad ones too. I still stay in touch with a bunch of Army helicopter gunners and their crews, the 334th Armed Helicopters, who made me an honorary member.

Two weeks before the war ended, I was flying seven 105 Howitzers into Bien Hoa on a C-141. This is a picture of the plane that I flew. Each gun was on wheels and weighed 2,495 lbs. I had many flights into Vietnam. They were mostly airvac and refugee missions. My worst experience was bringing human remains back from Vietnam. They were stacked up from the front of the plane to the back, all 70 feet. Then in the midst of it all and during the fall of Vietnam, we were doing baby lifts out of Nam and people lifts from Nam to Guam. After the end of the war, the homecoming was bad. There were protesters at the airport. The police escorted us through a private entrance.

As far talking to my family, the subject has never come up. We do not talk much about the past. My son Doug is pictured on the right with my grandson. Doug was in the Navy from 1991 to 1999. He was an Engine man on the USS Taylor FFG50 from 1991 to 1993 and an Aviation Boatswain's mate, Launch/Recovery from 1993 to 1999. Doug was also on the USS Saratoga, USS JF Kennedy, and served in Desert Storm and Desert Shield from 1992 to 1993. The USS Taylor was based out of Charleston, SC and the USS JF Kennedy was base out of Jacksonville, Florida.

I guess it's all history now.

~ Glen Murdock, USAF, Vietnam Veteran

"
It was horrible how the people were to you guys.

My big brother was a Marine in the Vietnam War.

He was also hurt. He has scars and a Purple Heart and medals, but has never forgotten.
"

~ Sister to Vietnam Vet

Franklin Covington

U.S. Army

"I KISSED THE GROUND WHEN I ARRIVED IN SAN FRANCISCO."

My name is Franklin Covington, and I am a Vietnam Veteran.

My father is pictured here and served with the 121st Infantry, 8th Infantry Division, and fought in Germany and was near the Rhine River with the Red Army. The regiment went into combat in Normandy, France, July 8, 1944. The 121st Infantry Regiment participated in the Normandy Campaign, Northern Campaign, Rhineland and Central Campaign.

They were awarded the Presidential Unit Citation. He served 8 years in the US Army and didn't talk about it much. I lost him in 1992 and found out a few years ago that he won 3 Silver Stars. I am so proud of him. Dad was my Hero. I only wish that he had told us more. I think the war affected my dad because his temper was something we didn't like. He would pitch us up with one arm and blister our little butts. Dad purchased a farm in South Georgia, and worked hard to raise his children and provide for his family.

My two brothers and I served during the Vietnam conflict, as they called it. I served in the U.S. Army and was assigned to the 101st Airborne and 82nd, 3rd Battalion, Infantry 11 B 20, in Phu Cat, Vietnam in 1968. My greatest fear was artillery rounds and the land mines. After I came home, I would roll off the bed and slide under the bed if I heard any thunder. It took awhile to realize that I was back in my Land of Freedom.

Thinking of the times spent in Vietnam has brought back bad memories. I felt deserted and left to die by our Government. Every second of every minute felt like days. I know we had to experience the loss of our friends. That was the saddest days of our young lives. One day we were telling jokes or our life stories, and the next day we were crying inside. We were put in a country that we knew nothing about. The swamps and diseases killed many of us.

Our Commanders told us that the enemy had no leaders. They said their ammo wasn't good and this would be a walk through the bushes. We were also told that they didn't have snipers, and yet three days later, several of our men had been hit with headshots by a sniper. I felt the Commanders were trying to brainwash us, and I remember whispering to my friend and saying, "They have been fighting for 50 years and their ammo is no good." We laughed, but I know the majority of us knew better. Some will lead and some will follow. I think of the many experiences that happened to us.

My worst fear was land mines and rockets. I still dream of them and it is a fear that you can't win. I remember we got hit with the 120mm rockets and you could hear the sound in the air a few seconds before striking. It was May 1968, and it was just getting dark when we heard the sound of the rockets. They missed us by a few hundred feet and we were headed to our bunkers, running. I remember the sky turned completely red and the heat from the explosion picked me up off the ground, and threw me like a piece of paper in the air. The heat hit my face like a wind tunnel. I remember thinking, 'God, we got hit by a nuclear weapon'. I low-crawled into the bunker and I could hear, "Get your gasmask." The rockets had hit an ammo dump and debris fell like rocks pounding the ground. Our casualty rates were high and I remember all of us hugging each other, and preparing for an over-run from Charlie. He knew he scored big and they wanted to finish us off. We lost 17 brothers, and I will never forget.

The following is an excerpt from a letter that I wrote home to my family:

"It is Sunday night and 10 o'clock p.m. in Bien Hoa, South Vietnam. The guns are roaring and the skies are lit up with flares. Some of the boys don't care if they die. We need help over here. The blood is running too freely and fewer people care what happens. Some mother's son is dying this minute. Some wife's husband is charging a hill. He knows maybe half of his men will make it, but

the other half will be sent home. They paid their price and wasted their blood in the hot and infested jungles. Yes, they are soon forgotten, but we will not forget. Yes, it is war. At night we try to sleep, but we know something is going to happen. Where will the next rockets hit? God's help is our prayer. We are 13,000 miles from home, and we sit and think about our wives, mothers and fathers, sisters and brothers. What are they doing tonight? Are they thinking about us? Do they care? We know they do! But it feels like the Americans have gone to sleep and forgotten us. War kills, cripples, and blinds many people for years to come. The enemy does not want to surrender. We cannot fight this war forever. We are the strongest nation, 'I thought', but why so long in this ugly war? If I die here, it will be in a place where I don't want to die. I always wanted to die on the good American soil, not in a place like this, where they ship you home in a bag with your name and serial number on the outside of it."

I never cried because my dad would whip us if we did. I don't even cry at funerals. The internal scars are deep. With all of this writing, it is the first time I have talked about Vietnam. It is time to spill it and forget it. Easier said than done. But I am so lucky to read the stories of other brothers and sisters.

The reception returning home was okay for me. I kissed the ground when I arrived in San Francisco. Some beautiful lady ran and jumped into my arms and told me she loved me. I was planning on quite the opposite.

I worked in Law Enforcement for 25 years with the Georgia State Patrol with assignments protecting two Governors and dignitaries from various states. I retired and have my real estate and security company at present. My hobby is working with my horses. I also purchased 400 acres of land to develop a resort for children of deceased Veterans and Law Enforcement, to have summer vacations free of charge. I am currently working on the website for the resort to be called Three Forks Mountain, with a 35-acre lake on the property, which backs up to the Talladega National Forest in Fruithurst, Alabama.

The opening is scheduled for the summer of 2016.

-Franklin Covington, U.S. Army, Vietnam Veteran

"
It's truly great to see how the troops are received today.

While I was in Vietnam, a drunk driver killed my mom back in the states. When I came home, nobody was left to meet me at the airport. It was pretty sad. While going to baggage I could hear the negative remarks.

When I got married, my wife found a box in the closet containing my medals and other items from Vietnam. She asked why I had put them there.

My answer was, "I don't want anyone to know."

~ Vietnam Vet

JOHN GUS HASSLER

U.S. NAVY

"BEST TIME OF MY LIFE."

My name is John Gus Hassler, and I am a proud Vietnam Veteran having served in Chu Lai, from 1965 to 1966.

My father, grandfather and another brother, all worked in the defense industry at the Brooklyn Navy Yard, repairing war ships. The family would speak about their war experiences, on occasion. My older brother and uncle served in the U.S. Navy as well.

I was trained as a Heavy Equipment operator at the U.S. Navy School in Port Humneme, California. It is the best school in the Nation to train people.

I served in the U.S. Navy for four years as an active Sea Bee and was in Chu Lai in 1965 to 1966. The group picture was taken in North Africa in 1963 with me and some other Seabees at Kenetra Morocco, in Port Lyautey.

The first night as I was heading to Boot Camp by train to Chicago, the thought came to me, 'What the hell did I get myself into?' As I was heading into the unknown for the next four years I was nervous and worried. It turned out to be the best experience of my life. I had many priceless experiences. I still remember the foreign nationals and the men that I met and served with, and the countries I had the good fortune to visit. Whenever I run into a Brother Seabee or a Veteran, it's a feeling of Brotherhood.

There was nothing I didn't like about the military. On occasion my wife of 48 years would hear me say, 'Best Time of My Life', and she would take offense to that. But my kids and grandkids like hearing the stories. As far as the war itself, it went with no end in sight. Our country was becoming divided and the culture of our great society was coming apart. I changed. The group picture of Seabees shows me second from the left, with Anthony Mennella third from the left.

Coming home from Viet Nam in 1966 wasn't as upsetting as the later years. The mood and the culture were changing with drugs. Lawlessness, racial divide and the anti-war movement were separating everyone. By the time we got home, it was a mess back in the states. I had thought we were going to need a military coup to make things right again. It didn't happen then, but it looks like that could happen now. After Kent State, I didn't know where we were headed and I never encouraged my kids to join the military after that. I never discouraged them either.

I began as an equipment operator in Morocco on shore duty for 18 months. The next two years were as an E.O. in M.C.B.4. They had schools where they sent qualified boots to learn a trade.

As a civilian, I have made a great living, working in a trade that I love, as a Union Crane Operator for the past fifty years. I was the Master Mechanic on the Second Ave subway construction. My son John, was one of the crane operators and is pictured here with me on a job.

We are both members of Operating Engineers, Local 14.

~John Gus Hassler, U.S. Navy, Vietnam Veteran

> **❝**
> My dad is a Vietnam Vet and to this day he still has some things he just can't talk about because of the memories he has.
>
> I remember Dad yelling and screaming out in the middle of the night from flash backs while he was dreaming. **❞**
>
> ~ Son of a Vietnam Vet

NICHOLAS B. SINOPOLE

U.S. ARMY

"IT WAS A WHOLE DIFFERENT WORLD FOR ME."

I served with the U.S Army HHD, 43rd Sig Bn., and the 1st Sig Bg.

My basic training was in FT Lenard Wood, Missouri in 1968 with AIT in Fort Knox, Kentucky. I was a permanent Party Mechanic F-4-1 Armor unit, deployed to Vietnam in October 1969. I joined when I was 17 years old.

My dad and all of my uncles served in WWII and Korea. I heard a few stories from them. This picture is of my dad in his Sailor uniform who didn't speak much about the war. He did tell me about being in the Pacific and part of the naval bombardment, on the islands during the troop, beach landings and about shooting down a Japanese plane.

I was always interested in the Army and watched all the WWII movies. I thought I would give it a try because I was always adventurous. I heard a lot of my neighborhood friend's older brothers joined and went to Vietnam. I felt I wanted to try it also. When I arrived at the 22nd replacement in Long Binh, the first thing I remember was the intense heat and awful smell. It was 2:00 in the morning and 80% warmer than back home. It was a whole different world for me. I had a hard time adjusting to the heat and hated it, but after a while I ignored it and just concentrated on my job in the motor pool. I was asked to drive convoy, and then I was hooked. I was always worried about an ambush, and had been through only two that were not meant for us. Just the same, we saw the death and destruction that it caused.

I remember how beautiful the countryside was. I had a hard time believing there was a war going. Most of the Vietnamese people were kind and didn't seem to want the war. As far as combat emotions, I got an adrenalin rush that wouldn't quit. One second I was scared to death, and the next I was doing what I was trained to do, While driving convoy, I was either driving a truck, or up top-side, over the truck cab with an M-60 machine gun, wondering if I knew what the hell I was in for. We passed bullet, pocked rock, on the side of the narrow mountain passes, and burned out hulls of motor vehicles that were blown up on the sides of the road from ambushes earlier in the month. I always wondered how many GIs were killed or wounded. There were very few guys in the motor pool that had anything to do with convoy. So I found myself a home for the 20 months I was over there. When it was time for me to leave 'country' and go back to the states, I felt like crying. I felt like I was leaving home and had to reprogram myself for my return.

When I returned home in 1971, no one seemed to care about the Vets or the War. After I got home, there was just my dad to meet me at the airport, no sisters no brother, just dad. Wow, what a homecoming! You just didn't talk about it. It took me a long time to open up and talk to family and friends, Now that I have been with other veterans, I feel proud that I served. I had two neighborhood friends KIA over there. One was in my unit. We served together and drove convoy together. I met a lot of good people over there, and for the most part I really respected the Vietnamese People. They had a hard way to go. The group picture is of me at the MCRD, Marine Recruiting Depot in San Diego attending my grandson's graduation. Michael did one tour in Afghanistan and is currently stationed at Quantico.

The time I spent serving made me like life a lot more. It's better to be alive than dead (old saying from the Nam). It gave me a bit of a hot temper towards certain types of people. But on a positive note, it made me respect professional jobs like firefighters and police officers. My dad was with the Ferguson Fire Department until his death in 1986. I am now retired from law enforcement with the Lincoln County Missouri Sheriff's Department. I am married to my 2nd wife and have 3 grown children all married with their own families. We live in the country. It's just my wife, her cows, my two dogs and me.

Life is good.

~ Nicholas B. Sinopole, U.S. Army, Vietnam Veteran

> "You served our country well.
>
> I'm so sorry for the disappointments in your life and the sadness you have endured.
>
> By you writing your story I am hoping it helps to feel the better moments in life."
>
> ~ Vietnam Vet Widow

Eric Lee Wooddell

U.S. Army

"A TERRIBLE LOSS OF HISTORY AND TIME SERVED IN THE COMBAT ZONE."

My name is Eric Lee Wooddell.

I served with the United States Army from 1968 until 1971. I went to basic training at Fort Knox and then off to Ft Leonard Wood for Wheeled Vehicle Mechanics school as well as Officer

Leadership training. I attended Ft Sill, Oklahoma for Heavy Wheel and Track Mechanics school and got my orders for Nam from there. I was with the A Company, 93rd Engineer Bn., Engineer Brigade and in support of the 9th infantry.

I joined the Army to get out of my small hometown in West Virginia. My dad, William Kyle Wooddell served in the Navy at the end of WWII. I never heard him utter a word about his time in the military but know he was badly injured when a ramp/door was let go and fell on him breaking his shoulder. He never spoke a word about it.

The picture shown here is when I was newly married and leaving for Nam. Little did either of us know the future pain we would endure. I was in Vietnam from April of 1969 to April of 1970. In Vietnam I worked mainly as a driver for tech supply. When I came back to the states, I was stationed at Ft Meade, Maryland. There I drove for General Samuel Coster who had been the American Division Commander in Vietnam. Being under his position, I ended up with the pointed finger of blame at him and several others, for that horrible deed done by our American Soldiers at the Mi Lai Massacre.

I have always had mixed emotions about the massacre in Nam. The fear level and the things many of our ground troops had to endure was an enormous undertaking, even for a fit man or woman. The worst part came down to loneliness. My wartime experience changed me. My tour of duty taught me to always be slow in actions and attitude.

My greatest fear was the unfamiliarity of Army life. My reception back home wasn't what any of us expected because of the flavor of so many different attitudes against the war. As far as readjusting back to civilian life, there wasn't any. You just had to continue on in civilian life as you had done before. However, the Vietnam War is still affecting me. Many years ago while moving from Lubbock, Texas, I carried with me only my clothing and things that I needed to continue on in my life. I had over 4,000 pictures of Vietnam, which were lost in the move. What a terrible loss of history and time served in a combat zone.

My truck was named Truck 5 Ton. I personally turned up the injection pump and would haul 70 miles per hour. The MPS outside of Long Binh ticketed me for that. It was hard to explain how the rig gained so much power. It smoked like a forest fire on wheels! In this picture, I am digging up the tail fin of a large Chi Com Mortar round that landed 14 feet from the head of my bunk. I had just stepped behind the blast wall when it came in. It nearly knocked me out.

It's been forty years now, and my jaws are still clenched. The following is a poem that I wrote.

WHY DID YOU LEAVE US

On highway QL-4 somewhere near BEN LUC
Slic & I were traveling in an ARMY truck
To Saigon & Long Binh picking up supplies
Riding in a country under a bright blue sky

These missions we shared were always great fun
we enjoyed what we did under the hottest of sun
Our souls were as one, our hearts were of rock
If we'd been able, we'd have driven round the clock

Unknown to us that day, long ago and far away
an act of hate would forever, cause us to pay
for an act of murder, by a man we'll call brother
killing a busload of people, a baby and its mother.

Suddenly in my mirror like a big train smoking
came a familiar green steel, that wasn't joking.
Quickly rolling by us PEACE was given by hand
& four soldiers shared ground, in this strange land.

Rolling on ahead of us was, a bus bound for market
full of people and goods & an unlikely TARGET.
As the TEN TON cleared, with its trailer and D8
Slic and I watched murder, motivated by hate.

As the giant did strike, the buss half its size
people got thrown out, crushed before our eyes.
Under the bluest of sky and the hottest of sun
coming to a stop, we watched our brothers run.

Climbing from our truck & walking deep into that HELL
Cries of dying people, are still clear as a bell.
Lying in its own blood a baby just barely alive
while its mothers crushed body, was unable to survive.

Remembrance of that day, has never gone far away
& I have often wondered, HAS SLIC HAD TO PAY?
Murder has nothing to do, with things done right
while haunted memories, pain brings many sleepless nights.

Thirty years have passed, since that awful day
memory has faded dim so purposely I now pray,
under BLUE SKIES & HOT SUN, often I see that bus
Think of those BROTHERS often, WHY DID YOU LEAVE US?

~ Eric Wooddell, U.S. Army, Vietnam Veteran

> **"** Thank you so much for your service.
>
> My father was a Vietnam Vet and was treated badly when he came home. He suffered from many problems after returning home. He was a door gunman. I'm not sure how he dealt with it all.
>
> It is because of men and women like you and my father that I get to live free every day. **"**
>
> ~ Daughter of a Vietnam Vet

JAMES ALFORD PETTY

U.S. ARMY

"I SOMETIMES FEEL FORGOTTEN."

My name is James Alford Petty, and I am a Vietnam Veteran.

I was drafted right out of high school and served with the U.S. Army from 1966 to 1968 as a SGT, E-5. I was a Squad Leader, based out of Fort Hood Armored Corps in Texas and was stationed in Củ Chi, Vietnam with the 1st Bn., 5th Infantry. At 18 years old, I was drafted for war. I am the recipient of the Purple Heart and Bronze Star medals.

Our squad would typically conduct ambush missions against the enemy about twice a week. One particular night two buddies and I were assigned to "ambush point" on the front line. We approached several Vietcong who were smoking pot in a blistering hot, dark, rice patty field. The three of us immediately opened fire on them and then backed down to hide out until daylight, which was typically done to avoid enemy conflict. This was the longest night of my life. The minutes seemed like hours. While hiding in the rice patties, we spent most of that night listening to men die, as they moaned and cried out for help. The next morning, we discovered that one man had not died and we had to shoot him again. It was in that moment with a big dose of reality that I understood what it meant to be drafted into war. My very last assignment with the U.S. Army was to 'double confirm' and document, a list of dead soldiers from our squadron. This task involved verifying and comparing dead bodies to soldier names. These are just a few of my memories and experiences that have profoundly impacted my life.

One night while out on an ambush mission, I fell into a Punji Pit. This booby trap was made with multiple sharpened bamboo stakes that were rubbed in feces to cause infection. In a way I got luckier than most soldiers, because I fell at an angle so only one leg took the brunt of the injury. Unbeknownst to me at the time, falling into the pit, the stake split into one of the larger veins in my leg. When out on an ambush mission, we would typically travel with a medic, so he stitched me up right there on site. I had problems with my leg from day one and it wasn't until I got back to the states that a doctor preformed a series of procedures to dissolve that vein in my leg to get me out of pain. Interestingly enough, the stuff the doctor used to dissolve the vein immediately caused the sensation and taste of having a copper penny in my mouth.

My 3 uncles served in World War II, Otis Petty, Emit Petty and Ray Petty. My father, George Petty Jr. couldn't serve because of a previous leg injury, but Daddy was always so supportive of us all. My uncles never spoke a word to me about their time in the war. Maybe I was too young or perhaps they just didn't mention it. But I know my uncle's spoke of war with my dad. He was their rock.

All the casualties were by far the worst things I have ever seen and/or been a part, of in my entire life. It is hard to even go there in my mind. The climate was really hard on us and so was the lack of support from our country. It was just disappointing and confusing. We worked so hard day after day and the days were very long and exhausting. My greatest fear was that I might never see my family again, or that I might break my promise to my mother and not come back home alive. My mother was the strongest woman I have ever known. When I got drafted, she fell apart until the day I returned home. I carried momma to war. She was in my heart and soul and always right there reminding me to come back home alive.

I strongly believe that my participation in the Vietnam War altered what my life could have, and should have been. Shortly after my tour of duty ended, I was placed on anxiety medication and have remained on it for most of my life. I have come to realize that some things just stay with you. For example, holding a fellow soldier's hand and telling him it's going to be okay while he is taking his last breath. This also included listening to your enemy opponents moan, for hours while they were dying of gunshot wounds that you were responsible for inflicting. I have asked myself, if I would do it all over again. The answer is always "Yes." It's yes, because simply put as an American solider, I was defending this great country that God has blessed us with. It was my job. Fate had placed me between my homeland and the enemy and I was going to represent my nation with honor. I was a proud American soldier, with the responsibility to protect the interests of this great country, which I love and that God has blessed. Like my fellow American soldiers throughout our storied history in previous battles and wars, I know the closing line in our national anthem rings true when we sing about 'the home of the brave.' I know because I served alongside admirable men of courage, many whom never came home.

It was our turn to be America's protectors. It was our watch, and our moment in time to ensure that the stars and stripes continued to proudly wave and stand for everything it represented. I am proud to say when called, I answered and shouldered what my country asked of me. I served the United States of America with pride and honor, along with thousands of brave and patriotic souls, so far away from home. We always called each other in the squad by their last name. In this group photo from left to right is Byrne, myself pointing to my name on the tank, and Douglas on the right. Both men were alive and still in the U.S. Army when I was released. We had a brotherly bond.

The reception back home with my family was amazing. They wanted to know everything. But I couldn't talk about it. I didn't want to. On the other hand, it felt like the media and public wanted to 'shame me' for what I was required by our government to do. I felt, and still sometimes feel, forgotten. I am still adjusting in many ways. That's just how it is. It's hard to explain. I love watching war movies because I can relate to them. There are many times I can't watch them, simply because 'I can relate to them.' The movie scenes can often times be very overwhelming for me.

I am currently retired. When I returned home from war, I was a little lost but eventually I became a Baptist Minister and I have worked in the church for most of my life. I have also worked with Hospice throughout the years. I feel extremely proud of myself and honored that I stood shoulder to shoulder with my military brothers.

They had been where I had been, and they had done what I had done.

~ Buddy Petty, U.S. Army, Vietnam Veteran

"
   I had three cousins who were in the war.

One was a pilot in Vietnam. The other two were on land. This is why I give to Wounded Warriors.

We must never forget.
"

~ Patriot

WALTER EUGENE PIERCE

U.S. ARMY

"VIETNAM VETERANS ARE THE MOST RESILIENT."

My name is Kay Pierce, and I am the widow of Walter Eugene Pierce, a Vietnam Veteran.

Eugene served with the 101st Airborne Calvary, Company A, the 199th LIB 3rd, and 7th Company A with 2 tours between 1967 and 1969. He was called Walter or Gene during his service years. Gene left Ft. Banning in August of 1967 for Vietnam and celebrated his 21st birthday in October. Gene was a sniper and part of a Special Forces group out of Ft. Benning, GA, called 'Red Catchers.' They were known as 'Light, Accurate and Swift'. They were undercover behind enemy lines and destroyed the enemy by surprise.

He told me that he was in Air Drop with the 101st Airborne Calvary in an air assault on Song Be. On one drop, he fell through what he described, as 20 feet of tall grass for a search and destroy mission. His troop went to the first house and it was empty. They approached the second house and it was empty, but they found a trap door, opened it and found it full of Vietnamese civilians. There were 15 people. They were old, middle aged, and young as they emerged from the basement. They had to immediately produce their 'papers' or the orders were to 'shoot on sight'. One man was shaking so badly he couldn't get his papers. Another soldier from his unit placed a gun to the man's head demanding his papers. But Gene intervened and said to 'give the man a minute'. The man produced his papers and was not killed.

One time he told me, "There is nothing to killing a man. I can kill him. It's living with the fact that you killed him that is the problem."

Gene's dad, a WWII Veteran was also in Vietnam with his son, working with the U.S. Forestry Service building housing for the South Vietnamese. Jay Cravens, the chief director of U. S. Forestry Service wrote a book entitled, *A Well Worn Path*, which mentions Gene and his father several times for their service during that time. His father was one of the last people out when the war ended. He saved many South Vietnamese lives getting them out on the last plane, or else they would have been killed as informants.

Gene is pictured here with his 199th LIB 3rd/7th Co. A. on the battlefield loading ammunition. He is loading a bazooka with live ammo and has a cap on his head with sunglasses on. His comrade in the photo is Stan Beloat. The other picture of Gene shows him with ammo strapped to his side holding a rifle. It's my favorite picture of him. It was taken on an Air Assault to Song Be. Gene received a 21-gun salute and 'Taps' by volunteers at Ft. Benning, GA, during the funeral service.

Gene was a hell of a man. His Sergeant Dan Ford, gave him a WWII rifle with bayonet, after some big battle. My husband was spat on when his plane landed in California. He never admitted about having PTSD, but he had it. Gene concealed it by making everyone else happy. He gave, and loved to a fault. Gene told me that he had to identify many of his friends at the morgue. He said that it was heartless and had a cold feeling from the medical people.

I was his third wife, and we had a long marriage. Gene taught me that Vietnam Vets are resilient soldiers. The media and ultra-liberal hippies tried to bring them down, but he persevered for 40 years. He was thoughtful, kind, loving, fiercely patriotic and loyal! I have no doubt were he here today, that he would be leading a cause for what mattered most, with no concern for his own life.

Gene's major at UFA was journalism, but he never got around to writing. Although he rarely spoke of the Vietnam War, his knowledge of history was remarkable and he told me so many stories of true events. I hope to put them into a book one day.

I was blessed to have known and love him and have him in my life.

- Kay Pierce

> **"** Thank you for letting us all live free.

You are an amazing brotherhood of love. To all of the men and women who served and paid the ultimate sacrifice, may you R.I.P.

God bless you all and the ones you love and have in your lives.

Peace and Love. **"**

~ Patriot

GRADY MYERS

U.S. ARMY

"MY SHORT, CRAZY VIETNAM WAR."

In the late 1970s, Grady Myers was an artist at the Boise, Idaho Newspaper.

I was a young, features editor. We went separately to an office party, where people were supposed to dress like they did in the '60s. My costume was a giant 45-rpm record. Grady wore fatigues and told entertaining stories about serving in the Vietnam War. I was fascinated. In those days, the military used a lottery system to draft young men. Most guys I grew up with had college deferments or high lottery numbers, and managed to avoid Vietnam. If they served, they rarely talked about it.

I asked Grady if I could write down his stories. He said yes. I stocked the fridge with Old Milwaukee, bought a cassette recorder, and got him talking. Grady Myers was an M-60 machine gunner with Company C, 2nd Platoon, 1st Battalion, 8th Brigade and 4th Infantry Division between 1968 and 1969. When I transcribed the tapes, I thought to myself: 'This is like "M*A*S*H', only set in Vietnam instead of Korea. Of course, not all of Grady's stories involved humor, or even black humor. People died. People suffered. He suffered. Grady recounted even the saddest parts, as if telling an adventure story. His descriptions were those of an artist and a reporter, detailed with sights, sounds, and smells.

Grady served as an M-60 machine gunner in the U.S. Army's Company C, 2nd Platoon, 1st Battalion, 8th Brigade, 4th Infantry Division, in late 1968 and early 1969. His Charlie Company comrades knew him as 'Hoss'. To put my interviews with him in context, I learned about what the Vietnamese called the American War. Grady had been 'in-country' for a few months at the war's height, when the U.S. had half a million troops in Vietnam. Desperate to keep the troop pipeline filled, the Army was taking people with physical and mental shortcomings who would not have been accepted normally, including Grady, an extremely nearsighted, 19-year-old. Grady and I produced a manuscript that I typed on an electric Smith Corona and that he illustrated with drawings. We also produced a marriage, our son Jake, a divorce and an enduring friendship. The manuscript stayed in a series of closets and packing boxes. Jake served in the U.S. Air Force like both of his grandfathers did before him.

When Grady was in his late 50s, he began thinking about the war a lot. Thanks to information he found on the Internet, he learned things he'd never known, including the fact that he had participated in a military operation dubbed Wayne Grey. After decades of separation from his Army buddies, he discovered that Charlie Company had started to hold reunions. However, he was never able to attend. Health problems had confined Grady to a wheelchair, and, eventually to a nursing home bed. He needed something to occupy his mind. So we dusted off the manuscript.

He propped himself up so he could see his computer and created new artwork. This time there were collages made from Vietnam photos he discovered online. He painstakingly reviewed the manuscript, adding details and more profanity. That's the way the soldiers talked. When I deleted some cuss words using the argument that they interfered with the narrative flow, his reaction was a begrudging, "OK", as long as you don't girl-ify the story with 'heck' and 'darn'.

Illustration by Grady C. Myers @

Grady vividly remembered many experiences in Vietnam. The emotions stuck to his brain like the red tropical dirt stuck to his body. He called it a time of 'intensive' living. He told his wartime stories, always complete with sound effects. His helicopter imitation was second to none. He did sometimes come down hard on himself. After he reviewed his behavior, described near the end of the book, he e-mailed me to say, "I'm finding I don't like Spec. Myers very much." To which I replied, "I liked the young soldier a whole lot. He was so ... human."

Grady was a man of contrasts, with big talent, a small ego, strong language, and a gentle spirit. His tough constitution was legendary, as was his own disregard for his health. A futile war left him in pain, yet he was proud of his military service. He was well acquainted with depression, yet all of his life, he made people laugh. He once looked at a picture of himself in Vietnam, in which his camouflaged helmet accentuated his strong jaw and big eyeglasses. "I was just a kid," he said. "Hell, we were all just kids." Now, Grady's kids have kids. When he died in 2011, at the age of 61 from diabetes and other maladies, I thought it was time to share his stories.

The result is a poignant and sometimes funny memoir, *"Boocoo Dinky Dow; My short, crazy Vietnam War."*

~ Julie Titone, Co-author with Grady C. Myers of *Boocoo Dinky Dow; My Short, Crazy Vietnam War*

" My dad fought in the Vietnam War and I'm so grateful for his sacrifice and courage.

He has had flashbacks ever since and can never forget the evil that he had to fight against as a young man.

I'm disappointed in our country for how we treated them when they returned. But I am glad I live in a country that treats our troops like the Heroes' that they are.

God bless our country and our soldiers. "

~ Daughter of Vietnam Vet

JERRY WAYNE HACKNEY

U.S. ARMY

"LIFE AS HE KNEW IT WOULD NEVER BE THE SAME."

My name is Kara Hackney, and I am the proud daughter of a Vietnam Veteran, Jerry Wayne Hackney.

Dad served in the U.S. Army from 1969 to 1975 with 18 months overseas; 12 months combat tour in Vietnam and Cambodia, and 6 months in Germany. While in Vietnam and Cambodia,

Dad served in both the 1ˢᵗ Infantry Division and the 25ᵗʰ Infantry Division.

Our family had several serve as far back as the American Revolutionary War and Civil War. More recently, Grandpa Benjamin F. Hackney, III was in WWII as a U.S. Marine and participated in the Battle of Iwo Jima. He witnessed the famous flag rising firsthand. Grandpa Elmer J. Rupp also served in WWII with the U.S. Army Air Force. My great uncles Ivan E. Crawford, Jr., Wendelin A. Rupp, Quentin K. Clotfelter and Lester R. Young also served during WWII. Great Uncle Jack Thomas Crawford served in the Korean War. Many additional family members have served.

Prior to my dad getting drafted to Vietnam, he was a student at a university. He went to college on a baseball scholarship and played amateur baseball, including in the Connie Mack World Series, multiple times. He had a lot going for him. He was a free spirit in every sense of the word, and his adventures and opportunities endless. He felt an obligation to serve his country. Little did he know the price he would pay.

It was very hard for my dad to speak about Vietnam, especially the traumatic parts. He suffered badly from PTSD. Dad was never the same after Vietnam. He would say, "War is Hell." He went into the war a softhearted, innocent, joyful, playful, incredibly ornery, athletic kid. He had seen little, of what evil existed in the world. He came from an upright and loving family. As a young boy, he used to bring birds home with broken wings and try to help them heal. He once saved an abandoned kitty that was rolled up in a paper grocery sack in the middle of the street, clearly put there to get run over. He had that cat for as long as his family could remember.

Dad's family talked about what a different man he was when he came home. He was a completely different person. He told one family member once that the war really messed him up, and he was having a hard time dealing with it. He was never again the same. He may not have fallen dead on Vietnam soil, but a large part of who he was died. His heart was forever broken and his spirit torn to pieces. His innocence had been ripped away from him. Everyone remembered him as the one always smiling and laughing, making light of life and just loving every moment. Then he was thrown into a hellish war, dropped in the middle of combat, and listening to bullets hit the helicopter he was to jump out of. The helicopter couldn't completely land because it was taking too heavy of fire. He had to witness men, who he had come to love, die right before his eyes. He saw for himself the unimaginable evil of the enemy. He did things he didn't know he could do, that he probably didn't even want to do, things that hurt his heart. He recognized an ability to fight within himself that I don't think he ever knew existed. His body, his spirit, his mind, and his heart were all pushed past the point of breaking. But he kept going, because that is what a soldier does.

A dark, heavy cloud hung over his soul for the rest of his life, and there was not much he could do about it. He was the best dad in the world! There was nothing more important to him than his kids. He would play with us as if he were a kid again himself. He could keep us in stitches with his jokes. And he never missed an opportunity to tell us how much he loved us and to show us so, too.

By the time he came home from Vietnam, America was at an all-time low of citizens supporting the war. His 'Welcome Home' was a rotten tomato in the face, followed by protestors yelling, 'baby killers!' Dad was so upset he went to the airport bathroom and stripped himself of his uniform and threw it in the trash. He laid down his life, as he knew it for these very people who now hated him for it. He knew and loved young, brave men who lost their lives fighting for these same people. It was unimaginable. He left one war in Vietnam, and came home to another 'war'. It made his dad cry, seeing the change in his son. Dad couldn't even sit down at the table and hold a conversation. He constantly had to be moving, doing something, keeping himself occupied, trying to rid his mind of that terror that struck him in every silent or still moment. It was a constant battle that he couldn't escape from, no matter how hard he tried, no matter how much time passed.

But the peace I have in his passing knows that he no longer has to live with that pain he endured every day since 1969. The last battle that he fought was against cancer, which ultimately took his life on October 30, 1997. I was only six years old at the time. I will forever miss his presence and long to have him here. But I know we will meet again.

I am looking for anyone who may have known my father, Jerry Wayne Hackney. I think he was known as 'Sarge' or 'Hack' to his fellow soldiers. There were two buddies of his who lived through the war, 'Dog' Harris and Paul Bullbear, 'Chief.' 'Dog' was a black man from Detroit in the 25th Infantry Division, and 'Chief' was a Sioux Indian from South Dakota in the 1st Infantry Division. Paul was known for wearing loud-colored Hawaiian shirts in combat instead of fatigues. He was an incredibly brave warrior who became a mentor to my dad in his first months in Vietnam. If any of these names ring a bell, please let me know.

I recently came in contact with an extremely kind and generous person who shared these photos of my dad, which I had never seen before. The first photo is Dad at base camp in Cu Chi, Vietnam, when he was in the 25th ID. The second photo was taken when he was in the 1st ID. He is on the right in the photo of him and another solider holding up the peace signs. He is second from the left in the group photo, taken on R&R leave.

A photographer myself, I love everything about photography as it freezes a moment in time to last for many years thereafter. A perfect example is my dad's photos from Vietnam. I had searched about all my life for these because Dad didn't bring them with him when he moved away from his hometown. These pictures are more precious than gold and will be forever treasured!

I have always had a passion for photography, since I was a little girl, and I am grateful to have a career doing what I love so much. I know that many photos I take will do this same thing for so many people in present day and for years to come.

~ Kara Hackney, Photographer

> **"**
> Why have I heard and read so little about growing up with a Veteran's PTSD? **"**
>
> ~ Daughter of Vietnam Vet

ERIC E. BELL

U.S. ARMY

"FAMILIES AT HOME, ANOTHER CASUALTY OF THE VIETNAM WAR."

My father, Eric E. Bell was a Vietnam Veteran and served with the USAR/173rd., Assault Helicopter Co. SP4.

He was a 'gunner' and enlisted voluntarily and completed three tours of duty. He was in the thick of it in the TET Counter Offensive of 68'. After a few months on the ground, 'in country', Dad decided he was safer in the air and said he would rather be shot down then die in the jungle. His enlistment was in September 12,1967 with the USAR and toured until 1970, remaining a reservist after until September 11,1973. The photo in uniform was taken in 1968 with the 173rd Assault Helicopter Co.

While a gentleman, a patriot, a poet and a joker at times, when he walked into a room his presence commanded respect, and everyone noticed him. You either really liked him or not. Most people really liked him and his charismatic ways. He was his own man, a ladies man, and a man's man. He was a regular Tom Selleck. Dad loved to mud wrestle with the guys there in the jungle. They would get rowdy. He never talked much about his time over there but he loved a certain tee shirt that my mother got rid of because it became threadbare. I won't forget the day the shirt was tossed out, or the hurt look on his face. He was crushed.

As a child I knew he was overseas but it seemed normal to not talk about it. It felt like a secret until the movie 'Platoon' came out. Being the eldest, he took me to see the movie. It was then in a theater, with so many other Vets and others, that I knew what happened to my father and his 'pain' that he carried so quietly around with him. Many men wept and many got up and left to get a breather. The movie had an intermission. It was too much. I saw my daddy, a man I was secretly scared of, not only cry and sweat profusely, but a human being that like anyone else carried tremendous weight, burden and guilt mixed with pride and was struggling. It was like something was exposed, a scabbed was picked off and was bleeding and it was a shock to him. I grew up in Newport, R. I., for the most part. Dad was from Caribou, Maine. The three of us kid's lived in a military town or community most of the time. So being with others that were military was not foreign.

My uncle was a Captain in the U.S. Navy and of a war ship stationed in the port of which we lived. He too served during the Vietnam War but did so at sea. My brother is six years younger than I am and served in the U.S. Army during Desert Storm giving out vaccines to soldiers going to the Middle East as a medic. He was able to stay at base in the states because of dads' service, earned him, or so I was told. My father had an aunt and uncle, both serving in WWII as well as my mother's father who was an immigrant from Portugal. He served in WWI. He felt it was his duty for a country that gave him his freedom.

I think the worst part of the war for my father was how it changed him. He had nightmares and fear of losing control. He did not want to be alone with us kids and told my mom when he got back that she shouldn't leave us alone with him. What a burden for her. What a burden for him. He was a strong person. He was a man, a husband and a father, but who wasn't afraid of his shadow or the shadows that plagued him.

He always played and horsed around with us and identified a lot with teens. He was a manager of the football team in high school. He was still a kid under that hard, angry and tough exterior that had to be suppressed. When I share with others some bits and pieces of his life, they say he sounded like a hippy when he came back. He wasn't. Many suffered from drug and alcohol addiction. Food would suppress it. Isolation was the 'norm', so we were never around too many crowds. My parents liked to go to music festivals and long hair and the smell of 'pot' was part of my life. At times my father wrestled with suicide. I caught him when I was a teen, ready to take his own life. He carried tremendous guilt for so many things. Men, a lot of men, feel and believe that they have to fix everything that is broken. He was so broken inside. But there was no help being offered for that. We all suffered like so many other families. Our families at home became another casualty of the Vietnam War.

Dad was a police officer for quite some time until the late 70's. He found his niche. He also served as security to the rich and famous. He loved it! He was proud of this accomplishments. It was the one thing that he could do with a pistol and not be told he was a baby killer or feel that he was wrong. He served in uniform with some dignity, pride and respect. Here is a picture of us when I was about three or four. He was a police officer in Connecticut at the time. I had just burned my hand on an iron that I was told not to touch. I remember that to this day!

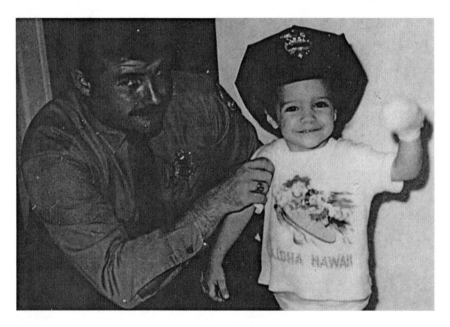

In his own way he started to come around and was making peace with God. He left us on May 17, 2011 on a Tuesday. As the eldest I, grew up in turbulent conditions most of the time. I was diagnosed with PTSD at 15 years of age. My dad and I had a conversation on the phone that shifted to me being the parent and not the child in a memory he recalled. I spoke up, and left it at that with him and gave him time to think about it. As his child, I did not speak up too much. I just did it and kept quiet.

After a week or so I had a strong impression and hunch to go and see him. So I went with my granddaughter and everything was fine. My father made sure and was intentional on giving me one of the biggest and longest hugs that I had received in a long time. He told me that he loved me. I believe he was saying goodbye. He knew his time had come and he left this earth as my father, a gentleman and a survivor. The Vietnam War tried to claim him. Like so many, they suffered diseases from Agent Orange, stress and being broken. He fought to the end and gave what he could in his own way.

Thank you Dad. You have taught me so many other things and left an impression that cannot be expressed right now...

I love and honor you.

~ Tanya Van Rose Bell

> " It took my dad about 39 years to get proper treatment.
>
> Sadly, he passed in 2014 to cancer when he was finally enjoying life.
>
> Give all Veterans the help and understanding they deserve. "
>
> ~ Daughter of Vietnam Vet

JULIUS "JERRY" DUANE WEBER

U.S. ARMY

"THEY SAY A SOLDIER OFTEN RETURNS TO THE BATTLEFIELD IN HIS MIND."

Dad enlisted with an Army recruiting station in early 1968.

He was only seventeen years old. Joining the service was a family tradition, and I guess he thought it was his time to go. My grandparents had to sign a consent form due to his age. He was quickly sent to Vietnam after his specialized training with the

U.S. Army 557th LE Engineering Company. He was listed as an Engineer Equipment Mechanic and Repairman. The medals received for his actions were the Army Commendation medal, two Bronze Stars and one Silver Star attachment, as well as the Republic of Vietnam Campaign Ribbon w/a device known as the '1960' bar.

Dad's unit supported the 31st Combat Engineer Battalion, 20th Brigade and the 168th Engineer Battalion. They built roads and were referred to as the 'Earth Eaters' for digging up the ground. They also repaired roads and worked on Highway 13, called 'Thunder Road' which ran through the village of Lai Khe, and was called by that name due to constant mortar attacks. These units along with many others were subjected to the toxic blend of herbicides, sprayed on the trees and vegetation that provided cover for enemy forces, known as Agent Orange. I know my dad developed several health conditions following his service, but issues related to this are not yet proven to be service connected after all this time...

I've been told by my relatives that dad returned from Vietnam, not only a man, but a changed man. They said he seemed to always be on guard and angry at times. He would often wake up from sleeping ready to fight. This 'changed' man was the only father that I knew and loved, in spite of his faults and flaws. He had a wonderful sense of humor and loved telling jokes. I'm sure that Dad enjoyed the USO shows with Bob Hope, when they came to his area in Vietnam.

They say that a soldier often returns to a battlefield in his mind. Dad was no different than anyone else and could not forget the past. Like many, he turned to alcohol. My father was only 55 years old, when he passed away on October 8, 2005. I loved him deeply and always will.

Losing dad caused the world to stop turning for me. I was in a 'dream-like' confusion, questioning how other people were still going about their normal lives. I wonder now if returning from Vietnam is a little like returning from any other war. Soldiers dream of going home, but when they get home they find it is not as great as they thought it would be. Things don't always taste as good as they remembered, and sometimes even the love they have or receive isn't enough to take away the burning and searing memories of war.

I have met many wonderful people through different veteran organizations. They have helped me get through difficult times dealing with the loss of my dad. I remember meeting another Vietnam Veteran at an event one day. I spoke about my dad's passing and shared that he had Post Traumatic Stress. Our conversation was brief and I walked away. Before I left the event, he came up to me and asked for a hug. He hugged me and said with a trembling voice, "This is for your dad.". I was speechless as I walked away and soon broke down crying. It was a healing experience for me.

His last birthday wish was for his family to find happiness in this life. I think my dad drank for comfort and he lived his life as abundantly as he could while battling Post Traumatic Stress and alcoholism. Through this tragedy, which had a profound impact on my life, he inspired me to help others.

I want all Vietnam Veterans to know that they are not forgotten.

~ Julie K. Weber-Torres, author of *A Daughter's Hero*

"
Thank you for your Service.

I have spoken to my father about joining the VA or support groups but he will have no part of it and has buried his Nam experience deep into his soul.

I feel so badly for him because I know he has a lot of pain and anguish over things he saw and did. I pray he someday finds his inner peace.

As for myself, I feel as if I am one of the lucky ones because my father came home.
"

~ Son of a Vietnam Vet

ROBERT JAMES BRANNON

U.S. ARMY

"HIS FINAL RESTING PLACE."

My father, Robert James Brannon, III, was a Vietnam Veteran who served with the U.S. Army for six years from 1962 to1968.

Dad was a helicopter gunman and mechanic with over 200 combat missions. While changing mortars, he would be shot at. He did not shy away from his wartime experiences and talked about them a lot. Once, he told me about a woman and her children in Vietnam. One of her kids walked up to his buddy and handed him a model toy, which later exploded and killed him. My dad then shot the whole family and barely escaped alive. He never got over it! He said that they couldn't trust anyone after that. They were in the jungle all the time getting men in and out on rescue missions. He survived 7 crashes and 4 gun-shot wounds. He despised Hanoi Jane and all of the non-supportive groups. It really annoyed him after getting discharged, so he joined a bike gang and was into drugs and such until he met my mother. She saved him from the gang and himself. Dad's grandfather and father served in WWI and WWII, respectively. Our ancestors fought in the Civil War. We have a weapon a weapon used in that war that has been handed down from generation to generation.

The PTSD eventually settled in from all of the shootings, which took a toll on him. His health continued to deteriorate both mentally and physically with the worst being the lung disease from Agent Orange. He was on oxygen for the last three years of his life. He really declined over the last ten years of his life. He lost his bike in a fire and then Mom passed away. After that, Dad gave up on life altogether. Even though all of his combat related health issues were doctor approved, such as PTSD, the hearing loss from guns and the chronic pulmonary lung disease and diabetes, (to name just a few from Agent Orange), he was denied 100% disability. This caused him tremendous stress as well as our family who had no means of caring for him. I knew of another veteran who was awarded 100% disability and was never in combat. I don't understand. Dad's health was on a steady decline, and he decided to shoot himself but survived. He later apologized to me but called me an idiot for getting him help. My sister called the paramedics who saved him. We had to put Dad in a nursing home at the end. He passed away in his sleep on January 22, 2015.

We had a special biker's rally with the Bandaleros, an elite biker group of Veterans on Main Street in Sharpsville, PA in May 2015. The starting line in the procession had 300. From there, the Honor Guard escorted his ashes to his final resting place at the West Side cemetery where dad joined his father and grandfather, both Veterans of WWI and WWII. Only one of his friends from Nam remains alive today.

My mission is to leave no Veteran behind and assist Veterans and their families, left with funeral expenses and other related costs.

-Robert Brannon, IV, son of Robert Brannon, III, Vietnam Veteran

> **"**
> Tears welled up in my eyes as I read these stories.
>
> My father also served in Vietnam. He doesn't talk about his tour.
>
> I am so touched and moved, and will be sharing with him in the hope he may also share his story.
>
> My dad is my love and my Hero, and I am 'Daddy's little girl' forever and always.
> **"**
>
> ~ Daughter of a Vietnam Veteran

KENNETH LANDFAIR, SR.

U.S. MARINE CORPS

"I HAVE SO MANY QUESTIONS."

My dad's name was Kenneth Landfair, Sr.

He was a Sgt. Major in the USMC and served from June 1960 to February 1987. He earned the Combat Action Ribbon.

His unit was the 3rd Pioneers while in Vietnam, which is now the 3rd Battalion Combat Engineers now. Dad's initial MOS was a Combat Engineer. As a LCPL his first unit was the 3rd

Pioneers Battalion now known as the 3rd Combat Engineer Battalion, which he accompanied to Vietnam when they made an amphibious landing with an empty M-1 Garand rifle. It was early on in the conflict. He served 3 tours in Vietnam. From what my brother has determined, he was in the Quang Tri province.

Dad retired in 1987. He had several medals, Certificate of Merit, Sea Service Deployment ribbon 1, Good Conduct (9), National Defense Service medal, Vietnam service medal 3*, Certificate of Commendation (5), Vietnam Presidential Unit Citation, Vietnam Campaign with device, M-14 Sharpshooter, Combat Action ribbon and the Meritorious Service medal. That is what I've been able to find so far.

My dad didn't speak at all of his time in Vietnam and wouldn't speak to my brother about his time 'in country' either. He told me he would tell me someday about his experiences, but that someday never came before he passed. When he died, he was a retired Sergeant Major. I never even knew that he had been in Vietnam until I was an adult. I have so many questions that were never answered.

My favorite movie is *When We Were Soldiers*. I've watched it dozens of times wondering if that's what he went through. I believe I was 6 or 7 by the time he made it home for good. My dad was also a drill instructor at MCRD. The story I was told by my mom about one of my dad's homecomings was that I yelled at him and told him to leave. I really have no memories from back then. My mom was also in the Navy Reserve. I miss them both so much.

This is a picture of my father in his dress uniform. The group photo shows my dad on the left and my Marine Corps Uncle, Donald Fisher. They are putting on my brother's stripes. My brother Ken Landfair, Jr. graduated boot camp at the same base where my dad was once a drill instructor at MCRD in San Diego. He retired as a Sergeant and recently told me that early in Dad's career in the 1960's, he designed the sound carts used at Edson Range at MCB Camp Pendleton in California. These carts contained a PA system to give range commands to the Maries on the rifle range. The carts were moved between the 100-yard, 300-yard and 500-yard firing lines. My brother said they were still there when he was in recruit training in September of 1987. Dad also told my brother that while in Vietnam the government came out with a new rifle, the M-14 and he had to give up his M-1. After instruction on the M-14, his unit proceeded to the rifle range to qualify on the new rifle. Prior to my father firing his new rifle, another Marine took his first couple of shots with the M-14 and the rifle's bolt housing exploded, sending shrapnel into the Marine's face and killing him. The Marines were then instructed to return their M-14 rifles and redrew their M-1 rifles. Dad was later told to turn in his M-1 again and commence using the new M-16. Although he maintained his Rifle Expert 2nd Award Badge throughout his career he said his biggest regret while in the Marines was turning in his M-1.

Around 1979, his last tenure as a Master Sergeant and Chief Drill Instructor for 2nd Battalion, H Company, MCRD San Diego, CA, he was moved to First Sergeant and was transferred back to 3rd Combat Engineer Battalion. He deployed overseas to Okinawa, Japan as the Company First Sergeant. His battalion proceeded to several islands in the Mariana Islands. Visiting Guam, Saipan, and Tinian. Their mission was to locate and destroy munitions left over from WWII.

In 1981 he returned stateside and was stationed in Fort Bliss Texas to attend the U.S. Army Sergeant's Major Academy. Upon completion of the course, 6 months later, he was transferred to 3rd Tank Battalion at MCAGCC, Twenty-nine Palms in mid 1981. He was the Battalion First Sergeant.

Dad served 6 years as a drill instructor at MCRD, Sand Diego and 3 years as a drill instructor at Officer Candidate School in Virginia. He also served in these billets as a Drill Instructor, Senior Drill Instructor and a Chief Drill Instructor. The fact that my father served for 26 plus years has made me very proud. I feel connected to every Marine. I would like to try and find someone that he may have served with.

In mid 1983, my father was informed he had been selected for Sgt Major and we moved to Portland, Oregon in October. He became the Sergeant Major for the 2nd Marine Corps Recruit District with, then, Major James Mattis in command; the same General James Mattis of the current Marine Corps fame.

Sometime in late 1986 the Marine Corps required my father to transfer to a Fleet Marine Force unit preparing to deploy overseas. No longer wishing to be deployed abroad my father chose to retire after 26+ years in the United States Marine Corps. He retired to Clackamas, Oregon February of 1987.

As a child, all I knew was that my father was a Marine. I had no idea what he did or what it meant, or where he went except to 'to work'. It was a job, like a plumber or carpenter. I was never told that Dad was headed to war. I remember how shocked I was when I found out. I wish that Dad had told me what happened while he was there because the things I imagine are horrifying.

I wish I could hug him and hold him again and tell him how much I love him and how I'm so very happy that he made it back home to us, not just once, but 3 times. I hold my family close.

I tell my girls everything about my dad and their grandfather.

~ Kendra Landfair

"
My father was in the Navy and served 2 tours in Korea and 3 in Vietnam.

But I will never know what he did because he took his secrets to the grave."

We took his medals to Hobby Lobby to have them framed. When they called and said they were ready, we went to pick them up.

When we asked how much the cost was, we were told they were already paid for by his service.

"

~ Daughter of a Vietnam Vet

JOHN MICHAEL CONNELLY, SR.

U.S. ARMY

"I LOVE AND MISS YOU WITH MY LAST BREATH."

It was 40 years ago that the Vietnam War had ended. My Momma told me about the day my dad's chopper was leaving in 1969. She also said that he was holding me in his lap and crying, as he watched the fall of Saigon on television in 1975. He didn't talk of the war much.

My daddy is John Michael Connelly Sr. He was born and raised in Mobile, Alabama in March of 1945. He spoke very little about Vietnam. He did speak of it a little by telling me that he was planning on enlisting in the military during that time. He was working for Naman's Foods as a box boy and would deliver groceries. He was recovering from hip or leg surgery when he received his draft notice. He reported to Fort Benning and was in the United States Army. His rank became Sp4 9th Infantry United States Army. He was 'in country' and worked in radio operations and carried the radio on his back. He was also in artillery in the Mei-Cong Delta. This is a picture of daddy getting pulled out of the mud in Vietnam.

He had several cousins that served in Vietnam as well. Although I do not recall which branch they were in. Daddy went to basic training in Fort Benning and then he went to a base in Seattle. From there he went to Vietnam. Daddy's nickname quickly became 'Rebel' because of his Southern accent. His accent was very noticeable. He spoke of his Aunt Mae sending him care packages. He enjoyed the honey, Kool-Aid, and condensed milk that she sent to him. His guilty pleasure was drinking these items. He spoke of having them tucked in a river nearby to keep them cool. She would also mail him the Mobile Press Register. He enjoyed reading that. Aunt Mae saved every letter that Daddy sent. I read them many times. Daddy made a friend while there, who was a young Vietnamese woman named Snow. He talked about how much he liked her and about them becoming friends. He spoke of his fear that she probably lost her life after the US Troops pulled out in 1975.

He didn't talk about his fear, other than his friend. I could tell from his letters and his reassuring our Aunt Mae that he was afraid. While he was there he became sick once. The medic thought he had malaria. But he recovered. He was injured in the line of duty and got shrapnel in his legs. He was to receive the Purple Heart. But daddy didn't take it because he told me that he only 'did what any other Veteran would do'. He lived with a lot of anger when I was younger. Eventually Vietnam caught up with daddy. He suffered from PTSD. He had severe nightmares and flashbacks. He was eventually deemed classified as 100% disabled due to the war.

When I was young, I saw much anger and hurt inside my daddy. As I grew older and he began to deal with his Post Traumatic Stress, I saw a man that was very proud of his service but hurt by some things he had to live with. Daddy's worst memory was of a child that had been frequenting their base camp. They were familiar with the child who was 5 years old. He came into the camp one day and then pulled a grenade out of his clothes. Daddy had to shoot the boy. This haunted him forever and he would shed uncontrollable tears over it. There was another incident where he and his comrades were out walking in the rice patties and a VC jumped right out in front of him. He had to kill the soldier at point blank range. It killed me to see the painful look on my dad's face as he recalled this memory. He was protecting innocent people from communism and the VC had no respect for life at all. It was a war where our men were made out to be the enemy by the media. Daddy didn't get the honor he deserved. He fought for South Vietnam and for our country but his mind and part of him stayed in those jungles until the day he died. I'm proud of my daddy for answering the call to duty, especially when others ran. There is one precious memory I have from a Veteran's Day service at church one Sunday. When the Army song played, I watched my daddy stand up full of pride, as the tears rolled down my face.

When he returned home from Vietnam, the first thing he did was see Aunt Mae. He didn't get a major welcome home. Daddy had trouble returning to everyday life. Sounds such as fireworks, the backfire of a car, or any type of loud sound made him jump. As I became older he began to soften up and deal with his issues. But his mind never left the jungles of Vietnam. Daddy and I became extremely close. He suffered from Alzheimer's the last few years of his life. However his only problem was not being able to remember the last 5 minutes. He was in the VA Alzheimer's facility in Biloxi when he suddenly became ill. He passed away due to Sepsis. I was at his side, holding his hand, and lying by him with my head on his chest when he went to Jesus. The war was finally over in his mind.

My life is blessed because Mike Connelly was my Daddy. He served our Country well and finally got his 'Welcome Home' on the day he went to heaven, on October 8, 2014, being the greatest welcome home of all.

And Thank You Daddy, as I love you and miss you with my last breath.

God Bless All of You that served.

~ Michelle Connelly Lovitte

> "   I am the daughter of a Vietnam Veteran.
>
> That war would impact my life like no other, and I was not even born yet. Back then no one had heard of Post Traumatic Stress Disorder, much less knew how to treat it.
>
> Dad lived with it. I lost my dad about twenty years ago to a heart attack, but I always felt I'd lost him before I ever really knew him. "

~ Vietnam Vet's Daughter

PHYLLIS HARRIS

"NOT ALL WHO SERVED
CAME BACK."

I vividly recall when my brother and his classmates were loaded onto a bus from school to go and see if they were fit to be drafted for the Vietnam War.

These were seniors and I prayed all day that my brother wouldn't have to go. It turned out that his knees kept him from going. But 10 more boys were found to be fit and were enlisted.

Not all who served came back, but all of my brother's friends served and all came home. They were changed and they were not at all the same happy go lucky boys they were before they went. They were fearful and so hurt. They all stayed around where we grew up, raised families and are living their lives. They have remained friends and they all showed up for my brother's funeral in 1986. They remain my big brothers.

While I greatly admire all of our Veterans, the Vietnam Vets are very special to me, because it was the one war that I actually knew boys who fought in it. It was on the news in our household every day. All Vietnam Vets have my heart.

Thank you all for what you did!

- Phyllis Harris

THE WALL...
A VETERAN'S VISIT

Names inscribed upon the wall,
Brings back memories of them all...
Fallen heroes who were slain,
Their sacrifice, honored, beautifully plain....

Name after name, I see the flames,
Vast sea of black, I see the flak...
Row after row, the battle grows,
Ammo they need, the more they bleed...

Viet Nam, so far away,
All the soldiers in harm's way...
Thinking back, another day,
Jungle thick, so many sick,
How can it be, they're calling for me....

Reflections of a bygone era,
Clear as a bell, as if a mirror....
Whistles blow, the enemy close,
It is night, one hell of a fight,
When it's done, we have won....

But what a cost, so many lost,
My friends, you see, all brothers to me....
I look around, the crowd has grown,
The names I see, so many I've known,
Heroes all, they held their own....

A young girl, she asks of me,
Why oh why, how can this be?
They gave their lives, that's plain to see,
They gave it for you, they gave it for me,
They gave it so all – all, could be free....

It's quiet now, but people weep,
A silent prayer, for soldiers who sleep....
God bless you all, who answered the call,
You silent heroes of THE WALL....

Sleep in peace, the battle's done,
Be it known, that you have won....
In the Kingdom of God, your life, will never end,
For, it was you, who laid down his life, for his friends....

~ Peter S. Griffin, Vietnam Veteran and author of *Thoughts, Memories and Tears*
Company A, 2/502nd Parachute Infantry Regiment
Distinguished Member of the Regiment (DMOR)
Inductee 502nd Infantry Hall of Fame
101st Airborne Division
Silver Star Medal recipient
Viet Nam - 1965-66

ACKNOWLEDGMENTS

I wish to extend my heartfelt gratitude and a personal thank you to all of the Veterans whose stories appear in *Never Forgotten*.

By sharing your life experiences, you are helping Veterans who are unable to visit or talk about their past. They will read your stories and realize they are not alone. I know that many of you feel forgotten. You are not. This book is a tribute and testament to your resilience in facing the difficulties both during and after war. Thank you for your bravery and service, as well as protecting our right to live in peace.

May *Never Forgotten* be the "Welcome Home" that you never received. You will never be forgotten.

Welcome Home. May God bless each and every one of you.

~ Jenny La Sala

Helping Veterans And Their Families

Children of Fallen Patriots Foundation
www.fallenpatriots.org

National Center for PTSD
http://www.ptsd.va.gov/PTSD/public/PTSD-overview/basics/index.asp

Wounded Warriors In Action
www.wwiaf.org

22 Must Stop Suicides
www.22muststop.org

Operation First Response
www.operationfirstresponse.org

Wounded Warrior Project
www.woundedwarriorproject.org

Fisher House Foundation
www.fisherhouse.org

National Military Family Association
www.militaryfamily.org

Special Operations Warrior Foundation
www.specialops.org

Women in military Service for America Memorial Foundation
www.womensmemorial.org/About/welcome.html

HOTLINE FOR VETERANS, THEIR FAMILY MEMBERS AND FRIENDS: For Confidential Support Call 1-800-273-8255 (PRESS 1)

CAREGIVER SUPPORT HELPLINE FOR ALL VETERANS: For Emotional Support, Referrals, Etc. Call: 1-855-260-3274

FOR WOMEN VETERANS: For Help And Information On Benefits, Etc. Call 1-800-829-6636

Historian Editor: Dr. Erik B. Villard, Director of the VietnamWarHistoryOrg on Facebook

Editor: Karen Wright, USAF Veteran and Director of Honor and Remember New York Chapter and on Facebook

For comments or sharing military stories, please visit Jenny La Sala's Veteran Tribute Facebook page, Comes A Soldier's Whisper and/or website www.JennyLasala.com

Front cover photos:
Buddy Petty
Walter Eugene Pierce
Larry Schnitzler-Spriggs

Back cover photo:
Dennis Sprague

CPSIA information can be obtained
at www.ICGtesting.com
Printed in the USA
FSOW02n0203070217
30473FS

9 781490 766423